In a Nutshell
Articles and Opinions during South Sudanese Civil War
Part 2

Chuar Juet Jock

ISBN-13:
978-1542494083

ISBN-10:
1542494087

DEDICATION

To my mom Nyakong Lual Jock, my sister Nyandot and
my grandmother Nyamoun whose love has been the
source of nourishment and motivation.
To my Kids, Jal, Goar, Nyakong and Nyamoun Chuar
Love you all

CONTENTS

PREFACE

This is the second book of my opinion articles 'In a Nutshell" that I publish regularly on my Facebook's timeline and where I thoroughly offers my own opinions and analysis on the current South Sudanese civil war that have started in 2013 as a result of the political rift within the ruling party, the SPLM and which immediately was diverted to be a tribal war between the main dominant tribes of South Sudan, the Dinka and Nuer. Subsequently, the Juba Nuer massacres, was the initial cause of why the war went tribal, it was also a necessary evil for Mr. Salva Kiir to break his imminent democratic replacement within his own SPLM political bureau and in which the majority members siding with Dr. Riek Machar and were in favor of replacing him if the party have to hold its leadership election before the projected national election in 2015. Well, the reality is, those who want to destroy South Sudan simply won't need a lot of thinking and conspiracy theory than the setting of the two tribes, the Dinka and Nuer against each other and tomorrow there will be no such a thing as South Sudan and on the other hand, the same context apply to those who want South Sudan to have a permanent stability, peace and prosperity. They must ensure the two tribes are in peace, harmony, equally and fairly recognized and this doesn't mean it should be done on the expenses of the other 62 South Sudanese nationalities. South Sudan must be inclusive, democratic and a country for all its people and for it to be at peace with herself before her regional neighbors and the world. After the independence in 2011, part of SPLM party and particularly those of Torit faction who based on 1991 split has grown a very radical and wrong concept, seeing themselves as the patriots and the those who have been defecting between time and another as traitors 'Nyagats", were feeling it is a time to arrange the political order in the country on a new basis and where they should be in complete control and also to start punishing and isolating those they have been accusing of treason, friendly forces to the enemy and collaborating and working with the North during liberation war and accordingly these so-called patriots "on their own perception of what patriotism is" started dismantling the accords and agreements which they have reached with the same South Sudanese political and military forces in order to reach a successful referendum and independence such forces of Gen. Paulino Matip, Anya Anya 2, South Sudan Defense Forces among others. After the referendum vote, I was one of the people who has given Mr. Salva credit for successfully bringing the South Sudanese house together in order for the independence to be a success. His political arrangements after independence were also accurate and were based on the balance of political and military power as well as the ethnic diversity and representation of various South Sudanese nationalities. Nevertheless, the nascent nation started with some grievances and rebellions such as that of John Olouny, George Athor and David Yau Yau that has troubled its promising beginnings.

Just only two years from its independence, the new country was at political chaos and path of tribal fragmentation and whether this trend was a result of the drastic reshuffle of his own government on July 2013 and which he removed his deputy and arch political rival Riek Machar and the entire cabinet or was it the persistent mismanagement of the country affairs culminated in rampant financial and administrative corruption and in addition to the insecurity all around the country as the then peaceful neighboring tribes were finishing each other as never before in bloody tribal wars while Juba, the capital became a theatre of unusual crimes and murders carried out by the so-called unknown gunmen. All these factors may have contributed in a way or another. However, whoever came up with the idea of the list of 75 corrupt officials and whose names never were revealed has definitely set up the nascent nation to a troubling political path which the nation still walking on until this hour.

A lot has happened since then and the real causes and the underpinnings of the 2013 political turmoil have been lost in translation, amidst extensive war campaign of propaganda, covering and smearing lies. Hence, it became a Dinka-Nuer war between 2013 and 2014 and in which the two tribes, defending their wrangling political rivals, Gen. Salva Kiir, a Dinka and Dr. Riek Machar, a Nuer fought each other in a bloody and destructive war that has appalled the entire world and humanity. There is no type of atrocity and war crimes that the two tribes haven't committed against each and which its main victims became the ordinary citizens who were subjected to all kinds of human's rights abuses, extrajudicial killings, displacement, uprooting, hunger, diseases that has resulted in high mortality rate and loss of lives and properties. It is estimated that around (100,000 or higher) South Sudanese have perished as between 2013 and 2016 as a direct or indirect causes of the civil war.

Between 2014 and 2015, the war has shifted slightly to have its original national face as other tribes became involved, mainly the Chollo of Greater Upper Nile and some tribes from the Greater Equatoria Region and Jurchol in Bar El-gazel. It is worth noting that the majority group which opposed Mr. Kiir in the SPLM political Bureau in which the political rift started were never a one tribe political group, they were a diverse group who were accusing Mr. Kiir of leadership failure, mismanagement of country affairs and lack of clear political vision. So being led by Dr. Machar, a Nuer, based on his seniority and the fact that he was the deputy of Kiir in both the party and the government shouldn't justify why Kiir decided to target the members of ethnic Nuer for one of the worse ethnic massacres in South Sudan history.

Evidently, in 2016, as the extent of ethnic massacres widened all around the country, it became obviously clear that the war was never a Nuer-Dinka war rather than it was a failure of leadership in which the tribal aspect was manipulated to an ugly extent. In December 23rd, 2013, I wrote this first "In a Nutshell) "I know that this war was at a store, that's why I never touched a foot on that state and also stopped writing on issues relevant to our country affairs when I have discovered that another monopoly is in the making. It was a war that has to be fought after independence to correct a wrong mentality that its results are what you see now. Living in a state of denial or twist doesn't do us any good. This is not about Nuer even though this is the running propaganda right now, this is about the system and the state, and if there was any good system in place and country that was founded on fairness, just and equal distribution of power and resources, and then we wouldn't be in this mess. But those in the forefront of this system and the state have been in complete state of denial and resistance to the calls and ideas to correct what we see as the origins of the state's problems. They see it as an attempt of undermining their total control of the state and its resources. I was just wondering how really we have fought Khartoum and why just to find ourselves in a more oppressive system and state and this time in the name of the tribe. If South Sudan has to be saved, and then let us honestly point out where the problem lies"

In April 2016, Mr. Machar arrived Juba to implement the ARCSS agreement which both signed on August 2015, unfortunately, within two months, the agreement faltered like no other, and Mr. Machar has to leave for his life while he was replaced through a conspiracy between his own aides Taban Deng Gai and Kiir and which ushered to a birth of new political reality which you will find more details about as you read through this book.

Chuar Juet Jock

ACKNOWLEDGMENTS

It is the encouragement and motivation that one finds in friends like all of you whether in real life, Facebook and other walks of life that keep me writing, keep me going and make life worth living. My appreciation to all of you.

Chuar Juet Jock

2016 ARTICLES

March 24,2016
In a Nutshell

The public opinion is expecting a beautiful foreign affairs' minister to an ugly government and a truthful spokesperson to a government that's built on lies and deception, well that's irrelevant and unrealistic. There is no way Mr. Marial can be in contrast and in opposition to the very government he represents and anyone who knows how the bureaucracy in government works, won't disagree with me that foreign policy conveys the president policy or his government and not necessarily the minister of foreign affairs. Well, I knew about one thing Mr. Marial could have done long time ago which is either to refuse in first place to be a member of a government he deemed notwithstanding with his ethics and norms or resigned from such a government if he wanted to save himself and his legacy but just like all the rest of muted ministers in Kiir failed administration, he instead decided to stay and to play with all the sad realities and controversial policies of the regime in order to achieve his immediate interests.

I don't know whether Dr. Marial has submitted a resignation letter or he was fired abruptly by Kiir as a reaction to the infamous letter describing the still contested region and people of Abyei as "Sudanese". Well, I could be inclined for the first assumption that Mr. Marial has requested to be relieved from his post as a foreign minister. This simply because what the Kiir administration has done to people and file of Abyei since 2005 is even worst and ugliest than this Marial's mess and all in all, the

11

Marial's mess didn't manifest out of the blue, it is all about and in defense of Kiir of course and Mr. president is a no fool when it comes to his political allies who has sacrificed the precious in order to save him. Marial is for sure one of them and he definitely will have a comeback in a way or another.

However, whether Mr. Marial has gone too far or not, the Kiir government has no credibility whatsoever over the matter of Abyei that it wanted to save at the very last minute with removal of Marial, simply because the controversy and the complications on Abyei issue are direct products of Kiir survival tactics and policies with Khartoum and not necessarily Mr. Marial's. Well, Mr. Marial in this case, is a man who is serving his boss and he has done so very well and for us who may be celebrating of his removal, I tend to cool down myself that there is no big political fish here to be fried, first because the system and regime policies in its top echelon of power won't change because of Marial removal, in fact, the regime's ceiling and foundation represented by Kiir, JCE and all its underground pillars are but intact.

The policy and strategy over Abyei has always been dictated by the fact that Mr. Kiir and his base knows very well that they can't fight Khartoum over the issue of Abyei and that neither Khartoum has a single drop of will to compromise over the Abyei issue and that any escalation in the matter, be it politically or militarily, has its dire and immediate ramifications on Juba regime and this was ultimately said in the shameful rejection of the results of Abyei people referendum by Kiir administration in which they have voted overwhelmingly to be part of South Sudan. However, what puzzles me from those who want Abyei to be won or to be included as part of South Sudan is their lack of vision and strategy on how to arrive to that glorious goal since 2005. The JCE and Kiir government, who claims to be doing the ultimate interest of Dinka people, are also the same people who are plunging the country into internal wars and divisions, destroying the very unity of South Sudanese that can serve as the national substance to defeat Khartoum over Abyei and not only that but at all the disputed borders with Kenya, Uganda and Ethiopia.

I have repeated in many of my "In a Nutshell" writings that there is no single tribe that can defend South Sudan in the face of any external aggression neither that will be able to liberate Abyei or the rest of border disputes and that alone should convince the Juba government to refrain from its narrow tribal policies and shallow strategies that don't serve no national interest but looking at what Juba is doing to the rest of 64 tribes we can just sum the game up as that the regime in Juba has no strategy over Abyei whatsoever. Doesn't that tell you that this Marial and Abyei political uproar is no less than a matter of political consumption and a political soup without a single meat or bone in it?

The foreign policy of South Sudan on Abyei issue has been a total failure since 2005 and was subject to Kiir's own vision and not necessarily his ministers. Starting with Dr. Lam Akol and later Deng Alor as foreign minister who hails from the area, the Abyei file didn't advance forward not even an inch and hence the accumulated frustration of Abyei people through the years has its peak when a group of soldiers from Abyei joined the SPLA-N forces couple months ago and one may say that maybe even a good percentage of Abyei people has already inclined toward Khartoum amid the chaos and failed statehood in South.

Adding to the wounds of frustration, the recent successive events of sacking of Pieng Deng Kuol and Dr. Francis Deng and Dr. Luka Biong from their posts plus the rejection of Deng Alor possible nomination to the would-be foreign minister in the expected TGoNU are all but fresh to the mind and the question of course is what Benjamin Marial got to do with all that? The recent approach towards Sudan and the agreements on full cooperation, opening borders to trade and travel and then suddenly the political fury between the two countries, with Sudan threatening to close its borders again and regard South Sudanese as foreigners over South Sudan failure of commitment to the recent agreements. Isn't it better we ask what agreements and what commitment Sudan is asking for? Given the fact that, most of these agreements are not made known to the public and there is total lack of what are they for or what has been exchanged.

Well, my guts are telling me the Abyei mess is bigger than this scapegoating of Mr. Marial and while Juba is trying to contain the SPLM/A-IO advance and disrupt its close ties and relations with Khartoum, one must never underestimate the probability of our own leadership trading Abyei secretly in such dealings. However, if the sacking of Dr. Marial is the start of the end of playing with Abyei and its people in Juba cheap politics with Khartoum then that's for sure a good move. Nevertheless, it is still to be proven whether Juba has a change at heart or it is just one of its usual political rhetoric, time will tell.

March 31, 2016
In a Nutshell

Programmed to Die a Loser

That's a well-articulated response Cde Bol Ring. While I may share with you the belief that our failure in not making the expected success in America is due to personal factors as well as other reasons such as adjustment issues in our new country and the challenges of transition from a less developed world to a more complex and well-developed world and as you said, the concept of success might not be the same here as in Africa. While we tend to spend money and time unwisely and sometimes in attempt to win the love and satisfaction of our families, friends and other groups, it is likely not the same here.

The fact is, had we knew our way around and had a quick understanding on how the society and the system works here we could have made early successes in many aspects albeit those who have been looking for success has definitely confined themselves within those set goals such as education and business ownership. While I think, America is too complex for people who have no basic education as brother Majang G Yiel has pointed correctly to it, however, the question now of course is what about our children who were mostly born here and got their education in American high schools, speaking, writing and reading English better than their African-born parents and are well oriented here with the American society and the system, do you see them succeeding? If we give the benefit of the doubt that we as parents were less Americanized, less educated and that they have the opportunity, they have the education but aren't they failing miserably? Drugs, gangs, crimes and then jailbirds among many, what excuses can we give this time? Blame the parents, who for the last

20 years been working in meat and all sort of production hard jobs just to see a brighter future through their kids and after all that the kids ended up in drugs, gangs, crimes and wasted in jails for the rest of their lives. What future does this community have here?

This is what I call "programmed to die a loser" because after all this journey of hard work and hope, it is now to most South Sudanese families a zero-sum conclusion. If you have a teenage child you may agree with me at this point otherwise your hope in your young children shouldn't either fade nor give any of us a right to judge these parents that they haven't done their best in bringing up their teens children very well and disciplined nor it is a Gene or DNA of failure sort of excuse. Let us define the real causes of failure America in order to save our children and the future of the community here.

South Sudanese in America need to face the reality and figure out what future do they have here when their children are sub-merged in drugs leading them to crimes and then wasted in jails for no less than (5 - more years). Our usual philosophy of ignoring things and burying our heads deep into the sand won't solve the problem. On the other hand, Cde Kuelville Ruon, Africa haven't changed a bit brother I think we ought to face the causes of our failure here and find the solutions that will make us integrate successfully in American society and succeed within American system instead of running back to Africa and that also may empower us to help our people back home.

April 5, 2016

In a Nutshell

I wish the silence of the political wolves and anti-peace elements in Juba and elsewhere is due to their final conviction that this country and nation at the moment need nothing else but peace and reconciliation and that nothing will overhaul the dire economic and political situation but a realization of an inclusive peace that touches every corner of this suffering nation.

However, let us not be carried far from the reality by this assumption and mere wishes, that the political wolves, anti-peace and the war- based interest groups in Juba and the region are finally for peace. War is profitable business to some as well as is the peace and accordingly, these wolves and peace woes need not mere assumptions and rosy wishes but a realistic approach and effective plans in place that will swiftly and efficiently deter and responds at any attempts to derail the peace efforts after the SPLM/A-IO has completed its return to Juba and that will reach its culmination by the return of its Chairman and C-in-C and the designated first vice president, Dr. Riek Machar.

Well, not everyone in Juba, the region, and international arena want to see South Sudan at peace, developing and prospering and it is of importance for us to assume that the anti-peace elements disguised in many masks and shapes may have a plan B that is worse than we may expect. I have seen some die-hard, regime supporters traveling to Juba recently, people who have an awful hatred to the person of Dr. Machar and only God's know what is in their heads. Well, let us speculate a bit on the possible moves of these political wolves and anti-peace, war-based interest groups in Juba, regionally and internationally.

First of all, I wish the SPLM/A-IO take its leadership

security and safety very seriously and this is no area for jokes and excuses. It has to be 24/7 and no off guards' lapses and holes throughout the IGAD plus duration and beyond. Efficient Intelligence gathering that's ahead of time and timely, probabilities of risks and danger and real preventive measures, screening, identification of holes and windows of risk and vulnerability, suspected groups, people and objects, well, these would be few of the many security measures that the SPLM/A-IO must have to survive and succeed in Juba. The underground anti-peace groups are at work and they shouldn't out-smart SPLM/A-IO security and intelligence organs otherwise their malicious objective to sabotage and derail the peace process and take the country back to war is high likely.

After the arrival of Dr. Machar in Juba and the official kick off of the peace agreement , the anti-peace groups within the administrative, executive and legislature bodies may resort to delay tactics, negligence and hindering of policies, provisions and decisions that are meant for reforms and restructuring of the ailing institutions, implementation of power sharing and resources redistribution as per peace accord and by such behaviors and actions, the anti-peace elements wishes to create new conflicts, difficulties and resistance to the roadmap of the peace process and to take the country back to war.

In another possibility, the anti-peace groups may resort in conspiracies theories, negative propaganda and sabotages here and there and particularly where there may be direct engagement between the forces of the SPLA-IO and SPLA-IG. Any single bullet fired by a drunken soldier could be manipulated and made to burn the whole peace process in a split second if no realistic measures are in place. Juba and maybe the whole country are still in trauma of Dec, 15, 2013 and it is likely that the panic and fears due to such irresponsible actions could widen to a larger confrontation. Our anti-peace groups are well learned in the ways and techniques of manipulating such incidents and hence the parties to peace need to make sure they have responsible soldiers and representatives at sensitive positions and locations.

The UNMISS must still be cautious and alert better than before and at any given time and space, it must have an efficient and effective plan on how to intervene and rescue the vulnerable citizens should the situation explodes. This time, it must be a comprehensive plan that must prevent possible ethnic based mass killings and possible genocide anywhere within the country and beyond. South Sudan needs a true work for it to get back to its normalcy and health and in which the race with time and against anti-peace groups should be a priority

In conclusion, the SPLM/A-IO as a champion of reforms and alternative better governance, good leadership must not be caught dirty-handed in any policies regarding financial corruption, nepotism in employment, tribalism...etc. This also may be exploited to the max by anti-peace groups and by its political opponents to trash the image of SPLM-IO and its programs of reforms and better leadership. Throughout the period of peace implementation, the public opinion will be inclined towards the leadership of SPLM-IO, how it performs in terms of service delivery, how it enacts the policies of reforms and how it approaches the issues of relevant to reconstruction and development at local, state and national level. However, the trend now is that the country seems to be divided into three forces that hires and accommodate tribally and which may be the norm and the tradition of TGoNU as each force believe, its share and representation belong to its tribe and its politically affiliate from other tribes. Such a trend is a gate for others to take arms in order to secure their tribe's representation and share in power; I wish the TGoNU doesn't operate as a government with three tribal heads rather than a government of South Sudan, by and for South Sudanese people. Let us hope all runs well and that peace lasts.

April 9, 2016
In a Nutshell

Make Dr. Machar Return Unofficial and Save the Country from another Bloodbath

Courage is needed at both ends of the current South Sudanese conflict, peace or war be it and the SPLM/A-IO has demonstrated that throughout the three years of warfare at the battlefields as well as at the search for a durable and sustainable peace at Addis Ababa negotiations venue. Hence, those who still doubt the return of SPLM/A-IO Chairman, the C-in-C and the designated First Vice President of the Republic of South Sudan, Dr. Riek Machar need to reconcile with that reality. He will be there as scheduled and of course, any delay or postponement of the date doesn't mean a complete reversal of his return to Juba. However, and given the magnitude of the enemy unknown plans and the sensitivity of the occasion, precautions and risk assessment must be taken very seriously and this may lead to delay or different arrangement in which it is understandable that the enemies of peace and the war mongers may resort to twist such occurrences and manipulate them to feed their ill intents. Well, they can dream on, at least in a world of unrealized dreams.

The return of SPLM/A-IO chairman is meant to end a war and not to initiate another war as the expectations and prayers of the anti-peace crusaders. It is meant to end the current bitter state of affairs in South Sudan, it is meant to end the suffering of South Sudanese within and without the country and I hope we have a way to have the accurate statistics at hand that tell us the sharp rise in mortality rate of South Sudanese everywhere due to war related causes; hunger, diseases, psychological and mental distress, insecurity, malnutrition...etc. The return of the SPLM/A-IO Chief is meant to rescue the ailing economy and the constant decline of our local currency in the face of dollar. Dr. Machar return is meant to end the bloodshed, heals the wounds of the tribal war and start the journey of reconciliation that brings back health and normalcy to our battered and wounded social fabric as one nation.

Such an occasion could mean a new start to South Sudan, a very promising one if we have learned the hard lessons we have seen and lived during the course of the bloody conflict. However, the enemies of peace and the war profitable interests based groups are in the opposite site of the coin and they may spoil it at our watch. You may agree with me that there are a good number of enemies to Dr. Machar return to Juba and with different various interests to an extent that I may suggest that the return need not be made official and popular due to the real and clear security threats that are present and I would suggest his return may need to be announced after he securely have arrived to Juba. Apart from the conflict of interest, the Juba government at this level can't be entrusted with the security of Dr. Machar neither it has the capabilities to prevent any security threats nor I may be fooled to the fact that SPLM/A-IO security and intelligence are all but enough to that mission. I suggest the international community, the IGAD facilitate the secure arrival of Dr. Machar.

In such a divided political street such as Juba and with all the tribal ego and tensions, the memories and trauma of

Dec 15, 2013 are still but fresh and alive and therefore such an occasion if made popular and public, could be another recipe for another bloodbath and a return to war worse than the one we are about to end. The significant of the Dr. Machar return is not the popularity of it rather than to bring this country and nation back to the gradual and step by step healing and reconciliation. In a highly tribalized society, and where the degree of tolerance, education and political awareness is so low, we must deny the possibilities of tribal bloodbath through careful planning and better alternatives and not through the assumption that all will just go alright or nothing will happen. The factors and ingredients for the possible conflicts are all but there but it is not for everyone to see. Again rescue the South Sudanese from another bloodbath by making the return unofficial and make the public celebrate it at a later date. We aim to end a war and not to start a new one.

April 13, 2016
In a Nutshell

The SPLM/A-IO can't avoid confrontations since the SPLM/A-IG can't avoid provocations

What are the reasons behind the detention of SPLM-IO media team? Were they behaving recklessly and provoking security problems? Were they authorized by the SPLM/A-IO leadership to carry out the media coverage for reception of IO leadership? If so, and then why the SPLM/-IO leadership is tight-lipped on the incident since yesterday, not even a single statement to cool down the worrying relatives, friends and supporters of movement at large? What such an attitude from the SPLM-IO leadership means to the security of the rest of the opposition supporters who have been campaigning against the regime since 2013? Are the opposition returnees safe given the negligence and carelessness of the leadership of its own media personals? What are the future implications of such behaviors and the continuous hostile acts from the regime carried by its agents in national security and other anti-peace elements? Will Juba government honor its commitments as genuine peace partner or will it continue with its unwarranted arrogance, provocations and bullying defiance? These are just some of the many questions that been worrying our concerned minds and hearts since the arrest of the SPLM/A-IO media team members.

The arrival of deputy chairman of SPLM/A-IO, Lt. Gen Alfred Lado Gore on Tuesday, April 12th, 2016 was regarded as a great step towards the march to the most needed peace and reconciliation in the country, unfortunately, the detention of SPLMA-IO media team has messed up the amassed joys and great expectations of our people who have then been indulged into fear through terror and then been pre-occupied with the safety and well-being of media team under detention of the enemy.

If the SPLM/A-IO truly means the business of change and challenge to Juba system of injustice, then the SPLM/A-IO can't avoid confrontation since the SPLM/A-IG can't avoid provocations throughout the peace implementation timeframe in the pretext of saving the peace. Given the persistence defiance, continuous arrogance and provocations that could have ended this shaky peace since August 17th, 2015, the SPLM/A-IO must take a harder stance if it really wants to get something to be implemented on the ground otherwise Juba is intentionally draining the whole provisions of CP2 and its attitude is meant to adhere to or to implement but nothing of the agreement.

Well, we have heard that the media team were calling out and mobilizing public in order to receive the deputy chairman and maybe later the chairman and then they were surrounded by the members of national security, beaten, arrested and taken to undisclosed location. No information about their location, well-being and safety until this time, however, the same source has disclosed that Gen. Taban Deng of the SPLM/A-IO leadership was informed about the detention of the media team members. Due to this situation that put the lives of the media team at clear risk, our expectations from the leadership of SPLM/A-IO was to release a timely statement briefing the members of the circumstances surrounding the arrest, their safety and when they should be released. Given their activism during the conflict and the persistence conflict of interest, the more they stay in the detention of Juba's national security, the riskier are their lives. However, the SPLM/A-IO leadership is still burying its head deep into the sand not even a high-profile leader has come forward to tell the worrying public, what exactly is going on, not even to assure us that the team are safe and sound.

I think if there is a mutual respect and effective communication between the signatories of CPA2, the SPLM/A-IO and IG, such a situation could have been handled without the media team members being arrested or beaten. However, if we agree that, public mobilization and reception is risky and unsafe given the fragile security situation in Juba, the media team could have been told through their leadership not to mobilize or provoke the public due to security reasons. They could have been ordered not to act in a way that will endanger the public safety and security but to arrest and beat them during such a historical event of receiving the deputy SPLM/A-IO Chairman and were all deeds and words of both parties are expected to usher the country into an environment of peace and reconciliation, the SPLM-IO and SPLM-IG leadership not only failed themselves but has failed to give the event its meaning and failed as well to appreciate the young men who were assuming they were doing their national duty in such a great day.

Mathematically, if the SPLM/A-IO is to continue to be the retreating sacrificing lamb and the SPLM/A-IG continue to be the advancing wolf throughout the peace process then one should expect a loss to the SPLM/A-IO in this uneven equation and unbalanced relationship at the end of the process. Nothing at the end will be left to the SPLM/A-IO, not even the post of the First Vice President will have any functions or meanings in reality. The SPLM/A-IO must stop the advance of SPLM/A-IG into its political territories, head on and at every act or provocation. Saving the peace is not only a duty of SPLM-IO but also an SPLM-IG duty as well and hence, we all must be ready to go to hell or agree to live in peace, period. An effective organization is the one that worries and care of one single life, safety and well-being of any single member of its base. The media team incident is a true test to SPLM/A-IO leadership and all its supporters are questioning big whether it will wait until another 1000 got detained, beaten, killed, demoted, humiliated, well, then there is no reason why the unfortunate Dec 15, 2013 massacre could repeat itself.

April 18, 2016
In a Nutshell

Our leaders' old grudges must die for South Sudan to live

With the return of Dr. Machar to Juba today April 18, 2016, we hope that the sad bloody chapter that started on Dec 15, 2013, is about to close and a bright dawn, a peaceful era for South Sudan and its suffering people is about to start.

In 2002, a similar sad chapter that started in 1991 was abruptly and inadequately closed between the late Dr. Garang and Dr. Machar and eleven years later, the old grudges and accounts power and tribal rivalry were unearthed again to be used against the same man, Dr. Machar by his same arch rivals within the liberation movement turned destruction movement. Well, this clearly tells us that, we don't have to fool ourselves that much because; the same grudges, the hatred accounts and the same men of all sorts of rivalries are all but here. Only if these leaders of old grudges are completely born again and decided to commit themselves to build a brighter future and reality for their country, nation, and the future generations and leave without a regret, these old grudges and hatred that is haunting them and the whole nation of South Sudan.

Well, I am not being pessimistic but rather than being realistic and arguing that we receive and welcome the new era of this relative peace ushered by the expected return of Dr. Machar simply because I think Dr. Machar is still a prime target of his old rivals and whether we decided to close our eyes to that bitter reality, it won't change a thing. Neither I am trying to indulge you into fears and suspicions that won't help us in the process of reconciliation and healing, regaining the broken trust and the fading confident rather than I am here, cautioning you that not everything in this peace agreement and its era that is about to begin is a milk and honey. Well, I think behaving responsibly, vigilance and caution are all but needed throughout the course of this peace agreement.

Those who may want again to hunt in the dirty political waters of South Sudan, those who haven't learned a thing from the conflict of Dec 15, 2013, and whose tribal ego and prejudice won't hesitate to irresponsibly pull a trigger of fire, here and there, and for reasons of that and this, needs to know one thing that this time and around, the conflict has gone behind Reik Machar and Salva Kiir or Gen. Malong Awan and Gen. Gatwech Dual but as we have seen throughout this conflict, it's the people of South Sudan that have paid so dearly and it is South Sudan that has been destroyed.

One fundamental reason that brought Dec 15, 2013, conflict was the notion of enormous disrespect to 2002 accord in the person of Dr. Reik Machar by the then Torit faction block. The 2002 accord was regarded and wrongly presumed as a mere gentleman agreement rather than an institution based agreement with a political and military backing establishments and that by the death of Gen. Paulino Matip Nhial, the imprisoning of Both Gen. Gatwech Dual, Gen. Gabriel Tanginy, Gen. Mabor Doal, and firing of Dr. Machar from his VP post, the then Torit faction that showers itself always with fake patriotism decided that it is now the time to show its real self and that it is time to trash the "traitors" and bring in the "patriots" and that's for Mr. Igga to be brought in the line to be the possible hire of the throne from the incumbent president Salva Kiir, unfortunately, the plan as projected didn't work leave alone that it almost have destroyed South Sudan and within days if not hours, Reik Machar, the rejected stone, will become again, the cornerstone for the unity of this country. Well, then the conspiracy in its entirety, will have to crumble and flatter like no other.

Well, we know and very well that with the return of Dr. Machar, the conspiracy is far from over and that, the Juba disguised, underground mafia and anti-peace groups are but up, tirelessly working again to undermine our peace, stability and prosperity again. Hell, we shall sleep and the enemies of South Sudan are awake, working day and night to undermine the peace of its people, the future of its young generations, and its potential of being the Dubai of

Africa. Hell, we shall sleep to let the political opportunist makes fortunes and build castles with the blood and skulls of our innocent people. Hell, we shall sleep. Welcome back Dr. Machar and to South Sudan and her beautiful people be the peace and prosperity.

April 19, 2016
In a Nutshell

The effective role played by the Gajaak Nuer of Ethiopia in support of SPLM/A-IO and to their persecuted Nuer brothers and sisters of South Sudan is remarkable and undeniable throughout the conflict of 2013. No one can imagine how things could be without that supportive role. Pagak, a town in the South Sudan-Ethiopia borders was throughout the conflict, the military and logistics base of SPLM/A-IO led by Dr. Riek Machar and in addition to that, nearly 2 million Nuer refugees are located around Ethiopia which is not only a second home to the South Sudanese Nuer but for all South Sudanese since Anya-Anya (1) liberation movement and accordingly, the two sisterly countries had developed historical, intertwined and well woven social and communal ties through time that can't be ignored.

However, the South Sudan civil war haven't spared the shared communities of Ethiopia and South Sudan and particularly the Nuer and Annuak of Ethiopia from troubles which were reflected recently in ethnic tensions in Gambella not than two months ago from the series of recent attacks against the Gajaak Nuer that has left around 200 dead, an estimated 50 children abducted and thousands of cattle raided. The assumed speculation is that, the attacks could be a part of reactions to the last month tensions in Gambella which are feds by the power struggle between the Nuer and Annuak on who should control the seat of governorship in Gambella but mostly is the question of what is the role of the invisible hand of South Sudanese government intelligence and its agents from the locals there in Gambella in exploiting such tensions to destabilize the region which it regards as the stronghold and the support base of its rival SPLM/A-IO. There is no doubt that both political opportunists in both countries of Ethiopia and South Sudan has been trying to increase the fire of those tensions for financial gains offered by the regime of Juba intelligence.

But what astonishing us are the reports that said the attackers are from Murle tribe of South Sudan and with evidence from some of the dead bodies of some attackers. This brings in the question of why would a bunch of cattle rustlers intentionally travel from South Sudan all the way to Ethiopia borders to massacres 200 souls and abducts nearly 50 children plus the thousands of cattle heads they have raided. Was it a planned punishment to the community that stood firm in support of Dr. Riek Machar and the SPLM/A-IO throughout the 2013 conflict? The timing and the surrounding events are all but points to the speculation that it may be a proxy work of Juba regime intelligence. Some of these so-called cattle rustlers are nowadays but sponsored thugs and tools that are being heavily armed and used to destabilize some communities deemed opposing the Juba regime. The thugs have a strategy of complete destruction objective and not a mere cattle rustling as they abduct kids after they have killed their parents and any elder or youth they find in their way. This is a complete annihilation attempt to the victimized community and there is no better definition of this kind of aggression but a complete attempt to wipe out an ethnic group. I hardly heard of Nuer people doing this to their neighboring communities even in their reaction and retaliation, I haven't heard about them abducting kids.

Lawlessness between South Sudan and Ethiopia borders must be addressed and I hope the Ethiopian government as they have indicated will thoroughly investigate and trace the origins of the attackers in order to identify the true motives and objectives of such heinous attacks and to bring the culprits to justice. The community of the victims and abducted children is waiting for answers, justice and accountability from both South Sudan and Ethiopia governments before they can take the law into their own hands and retaliate to bring back their abducted children and livestock.

April 20, 2016
In a Nutshell

It is irrelevant for Juba to deny landing permit to the plane carrying the SPLM/A-IO leadership just because of the claim that there were additional few personnel or some additional weapons out of what the security arrangements have permitted even though the number was still considered to be within the limit. Juba was well armed to teeth during the conflict and it would be a hit of stupidity to say that what the SPLM/A-IO is trying to bring for the protection of its leadership can be equivalent to the regime's arsenal of weapons of all types nor in terms of manpower, given the fact that the government was just relocating its thousands of forces with all their heavy weapons just some kilometers outside of Juba, leave alone whatever they have disguised as civilians, police or national security and other forces or whatever weapons they have in underground within Juba. Hence, the concerns of SPLM/A-IO that is causing the delay of their leadership can't be underestimated or thrown into trash bin without consideration given the fact that their main forces are distant away from Juba.

Well, the SPLM/A-IO is not coming for Juba invasion rather than to be part of the implementation of the peace agreement in which it has shown solid commitment despite many challenges and obstacles being provoked by the government and the anti-peace elements from here and there. To those who know, the government forces and the weapons in Juba and its surroundings are in fact 10x than SPLM/A-IO forces that are meant for protection of leadership should something happen in that hostile environment where defiance and arrogance are the norm and where trust and confidence are no more. Challenges to the implementation of peace agreement won't stop by Machar's return, as we can tell, in fact they will just escalate and be the norm throughout the peace process and chances for military confrontation are high likely given the fact that, the government and its supporters are still bullying everything and acting irresponsibly, provoking obstacles and hindering the process while in the same time, scapegoating Machar and the SPLM/A-IO in a campaign of smearing lies and propaganda and one may just wonders how they will change after luring in the SPLM/A-IO with that small force to Juba.

However, let us be honest and admit that any threats to Mr. Machar's security are without doubt a threat to this country's national security and stability given what happen in Dec 15, 2013. This country and nation is really charged with the issue of Machar and Kiir and regardless whether they are failure or success. Anyone who wants to trigger an endless fire may start again with an attempt to mess with security of these two leaders and hence the government must act as the first entity that is concerned with the safety of Mr. Machar and must rein in its own die-hards with their threats and bullying propaganda as a matter of national security threat. Mr. Machar now stands as symbol of historical rivalry and legacy of tribal show-off in the country political history and those who want peace may need to just swallow that reality even if it is not that pleasant to their tribal ego and political opinion. Peace starts with accepting your enemies and pledges a working relationship with them in order to fix what is broken.

While some are waiting for Machar return so the normalcy and beauty of life can return to South Sudan, some are busy digging holes of hatred and even praying harder that the return fails, well, I think we are still far away from being realistic and from the real issues that we have fought Khartoum for. The current unnecessary political noise and uproar has shifted our attention to irrelevant issues that hinder the nation-state building process and to what innocent South Sudanese truly dreams about. While I believe this shift is intentional from the current leadership in an attempt to create a system that uplift the standards of living of certain groups and areas and deliberately marginalize others, it is at its core and end results a failed policy and system that has brought us to this point of failure. Make no mistake about it, Machar will be there and face the challenges bravely and smartly, just wait patiently, we are almost there.

April 21, 2016
In a Nutshell

Currently, what South Sudan really needs is a national debate on how it can be inclusively developed and transformed and how a U-turn can be made from the past political mess and failed leadership to a one that is determined to make a difference on the ground this time and around, a one that should use the failed experiences of the past 11 years since 2005 to build a new reality and better living standards to the people of South Sudan whose their first expectations after CPA1 of 2005 was a complete overhaul to the miserable socio-economic status quo they have been in before and during the lengthy 23 years of liberation.

But you can't talk about a successful national debate or an inclusive transformation agenda that could effectively overhaul such a miserable socio-economic state when the leadership of the country is so divided and preoccupied with who among them should take the bones from the meat and manipulating the tribal divisions of their nation just to stay in power, doing nothing and delivering nothing for the past 11 years nor you can't execute an efficient national transformation agenda while the nation itself is divided and preoccupied with their tribal divisions and divisive leaders more than what they truly needs to make a difference in their living standards and the future of their children. Well, blame it to the leaders who deliberately created such a hostile public opinion and shamelessly manipulated every tribal division just to stay in power. A new formula is needed and Mr. Kiir, Machar, and Igga must provide this nation a new transformational leadership that can overhaul this shameful state of affairs and if it is not in J1 then let them dig somewhere just to get it.

11 years since the CPA 1 was signed and 5 years since the South Sudan independence and the only song we knew so far is Salva and Riek, Dinka and Nuer. Well, I think it is time for both of us with our Riek and Salva come to our sense and join efforts to transform South Sudan and make a positive change in our lives and build something for future generations. It is time to sing a different song of electricity light for everyone, clean waters, adequate healthcare, effective education system, inclusive security policy, paved roads and sustainable bridges...etc. It is a time for a different song and a mindset that can build a united prosperous peaceful South Sudan. The world that has been watching us for the past 11 years must be surprised and astonished on what we truly aim to. I bet they are about to judge us and maybe they are about to

turns their back on us or they are already about to categorize us as a nation and a country destined to fail.

Well, if we continue with the same current mindset and failed to capture the working underpinning factors of failure in both our social and political culture and foundation than we are for sure destined to a worse failure than the one we are in now. The magic is not that we can't fall but it is what we have learned from it and the 2013 conflict is a wake-up call to all of us that there is a serious need to change the persisting culture of failure in both our social and political thinking and that a culture of success and mindset need to be invented and oriented. Well, we still have a chance with the current peace hopes that a new era can be invented if we have learned and decided to change and commit to it.

However, the change we need is a top-down kind of change, it got to starts with our leaders down to the nation and if our leaders are still poisoning us with the same divisive political ideology of tribal feuds, then expect the worse, neither the national debate or action on transformation and development will be of success. Our leaders need to come together, work together, unite the nation, set an inclusive national socio-economic transformation and lead the nation to embrace such a noble agenda, I have no slightest doubt that victory shall be ours. "United we stand, divided we fall" (Unknown).

April 22, 2016
In a Nutshell

If the criteria of awarding a position in Juba government is like what is happening between David Yau Yau and Baba Medan in the newly created Boma state of Murle then this country of South Sudan and its suffering nation are in real troubles for sure. It is clear now the Murle has been used by South Sudan government intelligence not only in the recent attacks on Ethiopian Nuer in Gambella region but through the troubling history of former Jonglei state in which the bloody successive massive massacres were carried out against the Lou Nuer, Gawaar and Laak Nuer of Fangak and then the Twi Dinka in the then Jonglei state and later some areas of Eastern Jikany Nuer of Upper Nile state since 2006 up to the present.

Mr. David Yau was the first tool that has been used to stage such massacres until he got awarded with the Pibor mini-state in which he was made a governor in the wake of Riek Machar rebellion in a bid to use him this time on a separate mission against Riek Machar and particularly against the Lou Nuer areas and Fangak, Jikany and maybe Twi Dinka who are also presumed followers of Mabior John Garang, who stood with Riek Machar until this time. However, Mr. Yau, quickly acknowledged the change in balance of power and arms in the region and accordingly the immediate consequences of such a suicide mission given the last reaction of the Lou Nuer who amassed a huge military response as a reaction and retaliation to the massacres of 2006 that has claimed lives of thousands and aimed to uproot the threat of Murle to their area and people once and for good. However, it was again the peaceful leader, Dr. Riek Machar who advised the Lou Nuer people not to proceed with their mission and as a result, the Lou Nuer returned home but with one condition engraved in their hearts, should the Murle stage another massacre against their people then there is no slightest doubt, they will act effectively.

Given the fact that the Lou Nuer was the first region to be deliberately disarmed following the implementation of 2005 CPA and subsequently the first region to be deliberately and intentionally destabilized and prevented development services using the Murle as a tool by the same policy of Kuol Manyang in the then Jonglei state and in coordination with Salva Kiir in Juba. I have mentioned previously in my "In a Nutshell" book that this Murle conspiracy must be a well-calculated strategy between the state and the central government, using either military intelligence or the Murle insurgency. Well, the Juba Nuer massacres, which happened only days after Mr. Kuol Mana yang assumed his post as a defense Minister was the culmination of the plan, it was the start of its implementation.

Well, the subsequent reaction to the Juba Nuer massacres which the SPLM/A-IO were born out of its helm, has given the Lou Nuer people the opportunity to re-armed themselves again and I bet Mr. Yau knew this fact very well and as a result, he refused the repeated requests from Juba regime to stage new massacres against the Lou Nuer and Fangak Nuer. This has made Juba ineffective in that region and furious as well and as a result, Juba started to look for another dirty hand that can carry its bloody and malicious plans against the Nuer of the region and other presumed dissidents of the regime such as Twi Dinka and here come the dissolution of Yau Yau agreement and appointment of Baba Medan who until few weeks ago, proved how bloody and dirty he can go, sending his loyalist tribesmen as they were heavily armed, provided all the logistics and given the instructions of who to kill and what to abduct and loot . The magnitude of the Ethiopian Nuer massacre and all its surrounding aftermath, doesn't fit the pretext of cattle rustling by any measures.

The reward of course to Mr. Baba Medan is the governorship of the newly created Boma state in which they are fiercely contesting with the then Pibor mini-state chief administrator, David Yau Yau. However, the political rivalry between the two is about to expose the dirty hands of Juba intelligence and the regime's in its entirety in most of the tribal feuds in this country under the pretext of cattle rustling. The Ethiopian government which is currently carrying military mission within South Sudan territories to rescue its abducted citizens mainly children and women, won't stop short of investigating the origins of the conspiracy and the high profile culprits behind it and don't be surprised if some Ambassadors are declared as persona non grata.

Well, in a nutshell, the questions are: What Murle intellectuals can do to rescue their small tribe that its future and well-being is being endangered by such hostile actions and inhuman behavior such as the abduction of innocent children? How far can our politicians and political opportunism can go, sell and offer to Juba regime in order for them to secure a position? Is such a politics necessary between the people of one nation? Well, Juba may have taken the rule of Khartoum again and doing the same dirty politics of divide to rule and of course it is South Sudan that is being destroyed by such politics.

April 23, 2016
In a Nutshell

The question now is not whether Dr. Reik Machar and the rest of the SPLM/A-IO leadership will return to Juba or not, they will and of course after the Kiir government has shown us whatever power and brilliance they have got in all their delay tactics if in fact they have a drop or anything of such at all. Well, the question is what Dr. Machar and the SPLM/A-IO will achieve by being in Juba given these recent defiance and arrogance attitudes and behaviors of the Kiir regime? No doubt that such behaviors and attitudes will continue to be the norm throughout the peace process and timeframe given the nature of the regime and the nature of our tribal politics.

We may agree that the weakness of this peace agreement is that it has many enemies within the larger opposition movement alliance leave alone the government or Kiir political base at large and particularly those whose interests and positions are being threatened by the agreement. Those whose interests and objectives are not met from the opposition side are our brothers and sisters from the Choli Kingdom whose land issue in Malakal constitute a fundamental factor on their decision whether to be part of the SPLM/A-IO return or not. This depends solely on what Mr. Machar has promised to achieve upon return. Well, it seems there is nothing much Mr. Machar in his new capacity will do in that regard given the circumstances we already know. The Choli Kingdom and as the circumstances are imposing on them, they may have to opt to continue to fight the government in Upper Nile until Malakal is back to them or should the Kiir regime agrees on avoiding the country another war by solving this matter peacefully. As for the Equatoria front, it seems they will be alright with the deal whether as part of the government or the opposition and I don't think they have a major land issue as our brothers and sisters Cholloland.

The arrival of SPLM/A-IO in Juba and it being part of the government is a paradigm shift in both politics and life in Juba and the rest of the country. However, this shift will be determined and affected mostly whether the TGoNU shall operates with two opposing heads, opposite but in paralleled direction or as one government that must turn around the whole sensitive political, and socio-economic situation in the country and with a unified agenda of reconciliation and healing apart from the expected reforms and restructuring of the ailing institutions. We wish both parties can work in cohesion and unison to take the country and nation onto the safe shore and normalcy under the very watch of our anti-peace elements who of course will still continue to work in an attempt to undermine the peace process. Well, as long as Mr. Kiir and Machar are in agreement and coordination to serve the higher interests of the country and not stuck on their bi-partisan politics and interests all will be fine with South Sudan.

The JMEC and International community will need to step up their role and be effective enough in shifting the mode of the peace partners from warring and rival movements to partners in bringing back the country from the helms of war, divisions, and destruction. There is no doubt that there will be days of real tensions, moments of serious disagreements and differences and without an effective third party, such situations could escalate into major military confrontations that could threaten the peace process in its entirety and hence the JMEC will have to be as efficient and effective as the risky situation requires. Well, until the issues of land in Malakal and grievances of Choli communities and other communities around the country are thoroughly addressed; this peace is incomplete and exclusive. However, let us take the return of SPLM/A-IO as a step forward and work in a hope that the rest will follow in the direction of peace, unity and prosperity to our country and nation.

April 25, 2015

In a Nutshell

South Sudan is so blessed, the land is so vast, the resources are gracefully abundance and the people are so strong but what, we ended up after 11 years of our own government, the poorest, the weakest and the most failed nation on the face of the earth. Well wait, the real irony is not that sad part as you may think but the persistence notion and behaviors of the beneficiaries of such a mess that nothing is wrong and that this nation and country shall proceed with the same failed and dysfunctional status quo of "rob and run" corruption policies and lack of leadership. Hell no, enough is enough and it is the time to call spade a spade.

The arrival of General Chief of Staff of SPLM/A 1st Lt. Gen. Gatwech Dual and all his team of top leadership at both structures of the movement is a great sign for a new direction and a step forward to a brighter South Sudan in which peace, stability and prosperity should reign and enjoyed. The peak of such great hopes and expectations shall culminate tomorrow or next tomorrow by the arrival of Icon of peace and democracy, Dr. Riek Machar Dhurgon, the Chairman and C-in-C of the SPLM/A-IO and the designated First Vice President of Republic of South Sudan.

Well, we surely know that it is all fears to our anti-peace crusaders and war mongers while it is a great joy and celebrations to our peaceful loving South Sudanese people whose untold suffering increase and get bitter with every single minute of the delay of TGoUN formation and the kick off of the reconciliation and healing process. However, our anti-peace elements need to conquer their fears and all of us need to be courageous enough to embrace the new dawn, it is not all sweet and honey but it is the right thing to do and the right path to follow. Peace is the cornerstone of all the good things we want and dreams about.

Let us envision a peaceful South Sudan, where our kids play happily, goes to school uninterrupted and live a normal life for the rest of their lives unlike most of us who has spent most of their lives between the fires of successive wars or the helms of suffering in refugee camps. South Sudan is already an independent country but that won't be a reality without us liberating our minds and hearts from all the bias that are killing us and destroying the great potential of this blessed country. There is a great life, happiness, joy and success in a peaceful, united and democratic South Sudan for each one of us than in the South Sudan we trying to destroy because of our tribal ego, clannish jealousy and less loyalty and love to our nationhood.

This nation and country needs peace the most and our leadership must be above all the factors and reasons that are trying to hinder that. A long, lasting peace where long-term developmental projects and transformation programs can come to fruition. Let us join hands for the sake of our country and the future generations.

April 27, 2016
In a Nutshell

Welcome home Dr. Machar after nearly 3 years in exile and thanks and appreciation to President Salva Kiir and VP Wani Igga for the brotherly welcome and the positive change they have shown so far. All we need in South Sudan is peace and the rest will follow, there is no doubt about that but if we want a lasting peace then it has to be an inclusive sustainable peace, a one that is being sustained by deeds and words, by reforms and restructuring of what brought the war. Peace is not just an empty song that will just last without taking care of, without being watered on daily basis so it can grow, flourish and its dividend reach every citizen in the country. Peace is a huge responsibility that requires sustention, protection, monitoring, hard work, change of hearts and minds, change of attitudes and behaviors from negative and hostile ones to more positive, peaceful and friendly ones towards others. Peace starts with a single element within any group and that single element is either you or me.

Tuesday April 26th, 2016 will have to go down in the history of this nation as a day we were above our shortcomings and tribal bias as a nation and hence we came together as a family again to share the same streets, destiny, and future. Leadership has a very crucial role in any private or public entity and its failure or collapse is not an option because it could mean a real disaster to the stakeholders of that entity as we have seen in the last 3 years when our leadership collectively went awry and shifted its attention from its national duties and obligations to their cheap selfish gains, narrow clannish and tribal interests leaving the country and the nation to abyss of time and space, being kicked left or right by all the opportunists and business of exploitation and manipulation until we have reached to this point of nowhere.

The good thing of course about South Sudanese is the fact that they are strong people in the face of continuous ups and downs of time and space as our solid history has shown, what we lost, what we have endured and what have faced throughout our struggle were never simple but at the end we came out victorious and triumphant which reflects what type of metal we are made of albeit that's no justification for us to continue dying, to continue rock-headed, defiant, arrogant to the simple rules of logic and common sense while we are already an independent nation and country. What is the use of us being an enemy to our own happiness and success? It is the time we dance and enjoy being independent and being free, that's, we need to throw into the trash bin that mentality of war and bullying. Don't we mind being peaceful, development oriented and civilization conquerors? Well that's not weakness as some of us may think

The messages from both Machar and Kiir today, focused on how it is important for them to work together as one government and one leadership, initiate the process of healing and reconciliation, stabilizing the security and economy sectors, initiate reforms and restructuring in the ailing institutions and policy or law-making institutions. That's a great start of a reformed leadership that will surely deliver results and I wish they continue in that direction and it is not easy but it is the only road we must do the walk to bring our country and nation back to normalcy and health. Congratulations South Sudan.

April 28, 2016
In a Nutshell

As war ends in South Sudan, the policies and decrees that were made and issued during it should also come to an end. Those policies of emergency laws, the security crackdown on political dissidents, continued detention of political prisoners, and media censorship should be all but lifted. Peace should be reflected in all aspects of life in the new era and where our people can live, move and engage in the normal daily life activities in a peaceful, secure and healthy environment. If we have to expect a stabilization of our economy, then a change from war and hostile to a secure and conducive environment must be made available and new policies and actions must be enacted in which people and goods can move freely and securely across the country. The new expected TGoNU must meet those challenges and expectations head on, bravely and united

South Sudanese have lost the sense of security since 2005 due to tribal and clannish feuds, cattle rustling, inadequate security policies and enforcement and then came the disastrous war that has made the insecurity across the country reach its momentum. We have fled our country and our own made hell to either neighboring countries, UN compounds or the far Diaspora. The government which was supposed to be the one that should protect us, provide our security and safety became the one we ran from and fear the most and in other words, the public enemy No. 1.

While some may argue that the situation of war could have justified such policies, well, the new era ushered by CPA2 peace agreement must start with a bold and clear policies and actions towards regaining the public trust and confidence in their government and particularly in regards to insecurity and safety. A new substance is needed in our law enforcement and security institutions and personnel, a substance that serve the citizen, the country and not those people in authority and power positions. It is for our common good and higher interest of South Sudan, that we must place every one under the law and the first in that direction should be those who enforce the law and who are in powerful places to prevent abuse of power and the law and use it for personal gains and bias.

Neither the new TGoNU can stabilize the economy without adequate security measures and enforcement and hence, regaining the public and investors trust and confidence rely solely in on how safe and secure is South Sudan and whether the government is present and doing the right thing that is serving the higher interest of the nation and the country. There have to be policies, designed and enacted from the top, the government in collaboration with the know-how institutions and the private sector. Policies designed to achieve certain results within a scheduled timeframe and that must be managed and monitored in order for it to reach its intended end results. TGoNU is an emergency and recovery government that must work 24/7 to bring the country back to its feet and hence, task forces for different and various sectors must be formed and work effectively as scheduled and programmed, well, in case we haven't learned from our previous mistakes, the new task forces or committees shouldn't be hubs for financial corruption, nepotism and tribalism and then lose its goals and direction and hence, ends without delivering a thing.

Goods and people need to move freely and securely for the economy to boom and flourish, mutual trade between states needs peaceful communities and relations, paved roads and secure borders through policies and developmental programs which can be coordinated between local, state and federal governments. We have diverse resources in various states of South Sudan which can all be used and channeled towards a booming national economy. Foreign investors can't risk bringing their hard earned financial capitals to invest it in an insecure country leave alone that the war has damaged our reputation at the international stage and this will need a long term policy that is intended to regain the trust of the international investors and funding institutions. South Sudan has a great potential and vast diverse resources; however, the issue of security and stability is at center-stage and very fundamental to the realization of such a potential. These and those suggestions needs an effective and efficient government and leadership that plans, strategize ahead and act responsibly and we wish that TGoNU will be that government and leadership.

May 5, 2016
In a Nutshell

In his welcoming message to his brother Dr. Reik Machar upon arrival of the later in Juba on April 18, 2016, President Kiir said he wouldn't expect any opposition in any branch of the transitional government of national unity (TGoNU) and that all should work in unity to bring the country back to health and normalcy. While that is truly required in TGoNU to work as one government, with one president, and for one South Sudanese people and one Country of South Sudan as Gen. Gatwech Dual, SPLA-IO Chief of General staff has emphasized in his arrival as well in Juba. The need for unity is not only required by the different partners of the TGoNU but within all sections of the nation because without unity of will, vision and purpose we won't achieve none of what we all dream about and a comeback from the abyss of war and its sad effects will be nearly impossible.

However, working for change, positive change in our country and its ailing institutions and systems requires a different direction and substance if anything is to get any better and this is not an opposition and president Kiir and political base must accept this fundamental fact before they can attempt to override it and misinterpret this need for change to an opposition that may warrant whatever they want to come up with next to pull and add everyone to the status quo and the same direction and state of affairs that is causing all these troubles and setbacks.

No, there must be an opposite direction and formula to what is wrong and for things to be corrected and amended. This for sure will depend highly on the type of the approach from Dr. Machar and on the other hand to the extent of readiness from Kiir and Igga to listen and accept what is logical and rational from Machar proposals and demands. That's what will make the difference.

I insist that Dr. Machar must take a consistent direction and line of reforms and restructuring in all his proposals and suggestions to Kiir and Igga and to the TGoNU cabinet of Ministers and that must not be in a way that could be seen as political defiance rather than honest suggestions for the common good of the nation. However, for Dr. Machar, giving in is not an option and he may need to use all the peaceful and diplomatic channels, logic, and wisdom for the best interest of South Sudan.

Let us melt down the tribal ego for a while and focus on our common good, on the things that are needed to make South Sudan a great country and which we won't attain without unity and internal cohesion. Let us compete with the outside world as South Sudan and South Sudanese instead of focusing on our tribal competition and clannish rivalry that may at the end set us apart and ultimately set South Sudan on the path of weakness and failure as we have seen in the 2013 tribal war. Some people may just feel allergic to the name of Machar or Kiir or the SPLM/A-IO before they even know what messages each is trying to convey. The SPLM/A-IO has a great package of reforms that are good for everyone and it worth listening to them and debate them based on what is good for the country and what is not.

Great ideas may come from anyone and any political party and accepting or adopting them doesn't mean weakness or failure. Remember, this is our country and each one of us is fighting in his/her own way to make it something great and I wish there will be true friendly spirit and approach from our leaders of various political colors and debate all the issues of concern in a friendly environment with the aim to bring the best out of such debates. Good Luck South Sudan.

May 5, 2016
In a Nutshell

In his welcoming message to his brother Dr. Reik Machar upon arrival of the later in Juba on April 18, 2016, President Kiir said he wouldn't expect any opposition in any branch of the transitional government of national unity (TGoNU) and that all should work in unity to bring the country back to health and normalcy. While that is truly required in TGoNU to work as one government, with one president, and for one South Sudanese people and one Country of South Sudan as Gen. Gatwech Dual, SPLA-IO Chief of General staff has emphasized in his arrival as well in Juba. The need for unity is not only required by the different partners of the TGoNU but within all sections of the nation because without unity of will, vision and purpose we won't achieve none of what we all dream about and a comeback from the abyss of war and its sad effects will be nearly impossible.

However, working for change, positive change in our country and its ailing institutions and systems requires a different direction and substance if anything is to get any better and this is not an opposition and president Kiir and political base must accept this fundamental fact before they can attempt to override it and misinterpret this need for change to an opposition that may warrant whatever they want to come up with next to pull and add everyone to the status quo and the same direction and state of affairs that is causing all these troubles and setbacks.

No, there must be an opposite direction and formula to what is wrong and for things to be corrected and amended. This for sure will depend highly on the type of the approach from Dr. Machar and on the other hand to the extent of readiness from Kiir and Igga to listen and accept what is logical and rational from Machar proposals and demands. That's what will make the difference.

I insist that Dr. Machar must take a consistent direction and line of reforms and restructuring in all his proposals and suggestions to Kiir and Igga and to the TGoNU cabinet of Ministers and that must not be in a way that could be seen as political defiance rather than honest suggestions for the common good of the nation. However, for Dr. Machar, giving in is not an option and he may need to use all the peaceful and diplomatic channels, logic, and wisdom for the best interest of South Sudan.

Let us melt down the tribal ego for a while and focus on our common good, on the things that are needed to make South Sudan a great country and which we won't attain without unity and internal cohesion. Let us compete with the outside world as South Sudan and South Sudanese instead of focusing on our tribal competition and clannish rivalry that may at the end set us apart and ultimately set South Sudan on the path of weakness and failure as we have seen in the 2013 tribal war. Some people may just feel allergic to the name of Machar or Kiir or the SPLM/A-IO before they even know what messages each is trying to convey. The SPLM/A-IO has a great package of reforms that are good for everyone and it worth listening to them and debate them based on what is good for the country and what is not.

Great ideas may come from anyone and any political party and accepting or adopting them doesn't mean weakness or failure. Remember, this is our country and each one of us is fighting in his/her own way to make it something great and I wish there will be true friendly spirit and approach from our leaders of various political colors and debate all the issues of concern in a friendly environment with the aim to bring the best out of such debates. Good Luck South Sudan.

May 15, 2016
In a Nutshell

To equally celebrate with joy, the historical events such as May 16th anniversary or Dr. Garang legacy, we as South Sudanese must be entitled to the same rights and recognition and must equally be able to feel proud and live dignified as citizens of this country. But when some indulge themselves in tribal profiling and privileges attempting to create a first class South Sudanese based on tribal profiling and hegemony than the dangers are that our individual national contribution and heroism may fall into tribal abyss and risk bringing the would-be deemed national hero such as Dr. Garang back to his hometown or tribe of origin and the same to historical event such as May 16th, the day the SPLA were brought to existence to just meaningless event and in which celebration will be confined to those tribal heads.

The children, women and elderly in the devastated Leer town of Unity State don't see the SPLA and can't celebrate the May 16th anniversary the same way the SPLA's chief of staff Paul Malong and his Mathiang Anyor does. To the destroyed Leer town, seeing a SPLA soldier may indicate all the horrible possibilities of death, rape, castrating, suffocating and all the 2013 war invented techniques of ethnic based death. The same feelings are over the victimized regions of Malakal and the Equatoria. During the 2013 civil war the SPLA-Malong has done the forbidden even that the Jalaba of North Sudan during the 1983 civil war didn't come close in terms of heinous atrocities at large scale and on various types were committed on the innocent population of Leer town in Bentiu and are still being committed on sons and daughters of Equatoria to date.

Now tell me, what would May 16th, the day the SPLA were brought to existence indicate and means to some South Sudanese whose child was castrated, drown, sister or mother raped, fathers or brothers suffocated in those high heated shipment containers by the same SPLA? What would a celebration of the SPLA founder Dr. John Garang mean to such victims of the SPLA? That is our national dilemma created by power hungry politicians who, out of greed and selfishness, brought the SPLA the once mighty liberation army and which was created for a good cause, the liberation of Sudanese people, to just a tool for tribal domination and selfish enrichment.

Right after the independence I remember how were the heights, culminations and the peaks of nationalism before the 2013 war and in which I have seen each tribe was proudly celebrating the SPLA and its founders and giving them high regards of respect, heroism, and bravery recognition. I still recall some songs made in praise and rejoice of the SPLA's role, mightiness, and bravery by all the diverse artists of South Sudan. Sister Nyajouk Keat or Sister J, Duop Pur Dup, Nyapal Lul, Kang JJ, were few among many others who all have given great songs to the SPLA that we knew before the SPLA we have seen in 2013-2016 war. Well, given what happen in the war of 2013-2016, I don't know if they could sing the same songs now.

The need for a national army that its absolute duty is the protection of South Sudan and its people and regardless of their tribal differences, gender, religion, regions …etc. is of paramount importance to the national unity and cohesiveness. There is a need for an army that is conscious of its role, educated and oriented on what is its basic duty and that can't be manipulated by tribal politicians to serve their narrow interests whenever they are politically losing and this is also applicable to all the national law enforcement forces and national security agencies and personnel. No single tribe that can claim to own the national legacy of Dr. John Garang or the historical May 16th as they are national entities that belong to the people of South Sudan albeit those tribal heads won't stop surprising us and are doing an enormous damage to these national treasures.

Well, in order for such events as May 16th and national figures to be celebrated and regarded nationally, we may need to assess how damaging is our tribal concepts as individuals or policies ad government and politicians towards the nation's nationalism and unity and in a country where some feels alienated and strangers in their own country and society, the trends is we might not equally be proud of what is deemed as a national events or figures and It may need some time for the wounds to heals and to restore the damage done to our nationalism by the 2013 war and more than that, it will need a courageous leadership willing to put things right and in the right direction.

May 17, 2016
In a Nutshell

The very reasons we opted for separation from Sudan can't be allowed to be repeated under our watch in the independent South Sudan because as part of former united Sudan, South Sudanese know better what it means to subject a fellow human being to all sort of discrimination, oppression, subjection, and living as second class citizen.

It wasn't an easy to leave everything behind and to the bushes of South Sudan and to risk one's life and everything for the liberation of South Sudan and the freedom of its people. The beginning of second South Sudanese rebellion and Sudanese civil war was a justified reaction to the oppression and injustice of successive Khartoum regimes to the Southern part of the country where ethnic African, partly Animist and partly Christian lives. The Khartoum injustice was not at any form directed to any single South Sudanese tribe or ethnic but it was directed to all South Sudanese regardless whether you come from a small or big tribe and hence was the case when leaving Khartoum. The exodus of South Sudanese from cities and towns to the bushes of South Sudan to fight for their rights, dignity and freedom was so massive and by all tribes, small or big and in all walks of life as it was a direct reaction to Khartoum continuous obstruction of Addis Ababa agreement of 1972 which has given South Sudan more autonomy in the form of regional government.

However, after arriving to the bushes of South Sudan, many new realities emerge in the form of differences in liberation strategies, visions and who should lead the new rebellion and which has troubled the liberation movement from the very inception and has therefore resulted in enormous setbacks to the liberation struggle. There were two main groups within the liberation movement, those who want to pursue a direct strategy for a complete separation from Sudan or the "separatists" and those who think they can topple the ruling minority in Khartoum and hence create a secular united Sudan. These differences resulted in series of bloody confrontations between these two groups throughout the history of the liberation struggle that has devastated the manpower and the fighting capacity of one of the most powerful armed liberation movement in recent African history otherwise the fall of Khartoum or the liberation of South Sudan at the point of the gun was immediately at hand.

Sadly, these differences in visions and strategies on the liberation of South Sudan or Sudan were later channeled to tribal affiliation and another oppression and discrimination appeared to be in the making and this time in the bushes of South Sudan and in the name of the tribe. This in turn, resulted in mysterious assassinations, marginalization, and subjections of ethnic-based injustice that has forced many tribes to either to split from the main liberation movement, seeking help from the traditional racist and the jihadist enemy "Khartoum" to defend itself from the new tribalist enemy "SPLM/A". To make the story short, the significant of this narration is to dispute the false claim of some that the Nuer or other tribes have stabbed the liberation movement from the back and without justification why the Nuer or others left the movement at the first place. They want to feed you what you won't eat and when you say no, then you are a traitor, pathetic to say the least.

They talk about people leaving the movement but they never talked about the reasons and conditions of why these people left the movement. They weren't seeing anything wrong with their management of the liberation movement because they are the beneficiaries of their own created system. This is like that story of French liberation when the queen asked why the people are demonstrating and they told her because they are in need of bread and the queen quickly replied then why they don't eat biscuit instead. This is one of the South Sudan political dilemmas that has helped the true cause of the fight and independence to be lost completely in the mountains of nonsense, meaningless issues and debate. The fight and the cause have been channeled to the same square we left Khartoum for, who should rule Juba and who should take the meat from the bones, which should be the president, first vice or second vice. A debate and quarrel that's Indifference completely from the same reasons we went to the bushes and ended as the independent state. Until now we are in limbo, confused and divided in the sea of ignorance and the worse is that we are determined in that suicidal road and without the slightest chance that we may step back, consolidate ourselves and say no, we are collectively heading the wrong way.

Most South Sudanese in their diverse tribes went from Khartoum to the bushes voluntarily and to fight for the cause of South Sudanese albeit what they have found there is another oppression, injustice, and discrimination in the name of the tribe. Second, the liberation fight was never fought by a single tribe and the late former SPLA Chief of

Staff hero William Nyuon Bany who 90% of all liberated areas were liberated under his command can tell our today propagandists the truth behind the victories of Nasir, Jekow, Kurmuk and the rest of SPLA victories before the split of 1991. The question is how many areas were liberated after the split of 1991? If there are any than it wouldn't even come close to when the Nuer were part of the SPLM/A before the split.

Hence, why the Nuer and other left the SPLA in 1991 is justified by the very reasons that have destroyed South Sudan today "Tribal Hegemony". Therefore, one does conclude that the Nuer and the rest who left the SPLA during the struggle have no choice between two crocodiles and fires, the one represented by Racist Jihadist Khartoum and the one by Tribalist to the core SPLM/A and anything they have played between the two was for either a mere survival or self-defense.

May 19, 2016
In a Nutshell

Too late to return to Pagak from Juba and accordingly, the SPLM/A-IO may just choose to bury it heads deep in the sand of silence and non-resistance and to buy the expensive peace by avoiding a sure possibility of return to war with Gen. Kiir Mayardit given the defiance and arrogance of the later that we have seen even after the return of the SPLM/A-IO Chairman Dr. Reik Machar and the subsequent formation of the Transitional Government of National Unity (TGoNU)

As for the SPLM/A-IO, changing the regime from within that couldn't be changed through military means could prove to be twice difficult trying to make it possible through peaceful, political and diplomatic means and this is for the obvious reasons that Mr. Kiir is not here to satisfies his arch political rival Dr. Riek Machar and will not accept to give the later a win over him politically or give up his allies or the policies that have made him survive the nearly three years war and the campaign of Kiir must go. This has been clearly reflected in the way he kept his policies and decrees such as the troubled 28 states as well as his previous cabinet members and with Yau as deputy defense minister next to Kuol Manyang and which indicate how he intend to move politically and militarily should the situation erupt again. Well, read with me as I anticipate no big change in the general direction despite the formation of TGoNU and this could be reflected from the regime's bad boys' negative activities such as Mr. Buay Malek and the rest of the underground team.

Mr. Buay Malek is a good insider of Kiir political base and conspiracies planners along with his teammate Mr. Lul Ruai Kong, a member of the disguised underground strategists who plans day and night most policies and actions that are intended to weaken or destroy the Riek Machar led movement SPLM/A-IO whether through smear campaign of lies, conspiracies theories or covert intelligence operations such as the latest attacks on Gajaak Nuer, the SPLM/A-IO strongholds. Mr. Malek in real sense is not a just mere ambassador but a fundamental figure in the underground strategists of the regime that has been given diplomatic cover and cloth to plans and facilitates plans that are aimed to weaken and divide the Diaspora support base of SPLM/A-IO and particularly in the USA. Accordingly, he is one of the leading recruiters and defections negotiators and financials suppliers second to none but Tut Gatluak, the security advisor of Mr. Kiir.

So don't be surprised if either of the men isn't quiet yet or still active and at work, cooking new conspiracies one after another and writing all the smear media campaign or conspiracies theories that either are directed to divide and weaken the SPLM/A-IO from within and confuse the public even when we think that government officials like them should have abides by the terms of peace agreement which recommends for suspension of hostile media and propaganda activities.

However, in regard to either Mr. Buay Malek or Lul Ruai Koang, none is neither a lone wolf that is acting without backing or direction from the secret chambers of the regime neither none of them is a fool that is not aware of the fact that what he is doing could have clear consequences from his masters but in fact they are probably authorized to do so and this in fact very troubling because it indicates something fishy is in the making and that the SPLM/A-in –Government (SPLM/A-IG) has not adopted a new peaceful face and probably has a near future plan B that may caught the SPLM/A-IO off guard.

This claim is well backed by Kiir actions and policies and in which we haven't seen any slightest change in substance nor in the direction after the return of SPLM/A-IO Chairman and the subsequent formation of the TGoNU and which should mean a new era of peace and reconciliation, a new government with recovery, reforms, reconstruction and unified agenda but of no avail. Kiir is keeping his troubling 28 states intact and there are no indicators of any flexibility or slightest change in most of the controversial issues between the conflict partners. As for the SPLM/A-IO and aware that any direct opposition or harden stance on those issues may led to either political confrontation or at worse a return to war, well, the question is whether the peaceful and political approach towards those issues will ever work and change a thing or either the written protests to JMEC will ever be fruitful, well, not likely.

JMEC may proof to be as toothless as it may seem and its

mechanism of enforcement may not work at all with Kiir system that is based on defiance and arrogance and if they insist on punishing or pushing him to the edge, this could result in crisis that could bring the whole peace agreement to unravel and subsequently, a gloomy uncertain reality. Using the funding and financial package as a tool for pressure and enforcement, the Troika, and the International Community may succeed in some areas but I believe they won't choose a war with Kiir over peace, any peace whatsoever and hence and from a strategic point of view, it is either for the SPLM/A-IO to have no resistance and any say at all for peace to materialize in this country, a peace that means the silence of the guns and violence but not necessarily a peace that is based on reforms and reconstructions as promised because any challenge or opposition to Kiir policies will definitely generate a heated political debate and confrontation no matter how small or serious it is, it could trigger unpleasant outcomes and who could control that?. SPLM/A-IO has choices to make before it sinks completely into the vast ocean of Kiir Mayardit, well if they have any choices at all in the absence of effective enforcement mechanism to the peace agreement or where a return to war is not an option.

May 20, 2016
In a Nutshell

Gen. Kiir and base need to be nice and cooperative with Dr. Machar's SPLM/A-IO and not to use this rare chance of peace for political rhetoric and show rather than engage in serious process of changing our country for better. The approach to Dr. Machar and the SPLM/A-IO shouldn't be the way we are seeing it now, humiliation and insults and making obstacles and hurdles one after another and failing to create a conducive working relationship and environment that should encourage and motivate the country and usher it into a future of good and mutual cooperative working relationship and political partnership that will be best used for transforming our country.

However, I feel that Juba haven't welcomed and embraced the peace the way it should be and I believe the efforts that are being geared towards peace and reconciliation, whether they are local, regional or international should highly be appreciated and wisely utilized to the direction of change, healing, and reconciliation but it seems this is not the case. Both parties should be aware of a political front of anti-peace that has emerged out of sudden and that its aim is to frustrate these peace efforts and movement and divert it into a recipe for a new conflict and explosion. However, our anti-peace crusaders may need to conclude that, peace will also be the end of any new or future war and there is no need for those who are shallow in such a realization to waste the nation time and precious live in worthless wars and conflict.

It is a wrong start to think that Mr. Machar will give up about his agenda of reforms just because he is in Juba where some may think he already got his job back and then the rest for him is less important or those who thinks he is now trapped and may not have an exit should the situation worsen or just because the country needs peace and the people are highly suffering and then use such wrong thinking to humiliate Mr. Machar and his SPLM/A-IO , impedes the implementation of peace agreement and of course as a result of such a thinking, the regime and as we are seeing is going ahead with its unilateral agenda and without the slightest consideration of what platform the new TGoNU is formed upon.

Such a thinking is too dangerous and a recipe for a sure conflict, Mr. Machar and the SPLM/A-IO won't give in and even by an inch in their quest for reforms and overhauling of our country ailing system of governance and institutions. While the approach to such direction may change, the substance and commitment won't change. The TGoNU may standstill in some disagreements times, its meetings may be adjourned without agreements or outcomes but this should be a normal step in the process of peacefully, democratically debating and administering such issues of disagreement toward consensus or voting within the TGoNU cabinet or the parliament.

What will make the difference of course, is how such a democratic process will be managed and administered towards fruitful outcomes unlike those meetings of December 2013 that has failed and subsequently failed the whole country as well.

Mr. Machar will need to stand his ground as long as his political agenda and program of reform are sound, the judge is not Kiir but the people of South Sudan and the same should be applicable to Mr. Kiir if he believes the same way. However, both must refer to the democratic process and without resort to political bullying and those conspiracies theories of coup attempts as it was 2013.

Let us not panic despite the uncertainty and lack of clarity on how our country will proceed forward amid stalemate and defiance on fundamental issues that are important for the TGoNU to march forward and implement the provisions of the peace agreement and engage in tasks of recovery, reconstruction, healing and reconciliation. Our collective aim as a nation should be resolving the issues that are threatening the peace process and not to encourage a return to war nor resist the healing and reconciliation process. We must proceed forward as a nation and no matter how long we want to keep our grudges and hatred alive, our ultimate destiny is one and we must overcome our differences.

May 21, 2016
In a Nutshell

Our beautiful dreams in South Sudan are now suspended until further notice and the deal with this unaccounted time is that we must enter into a state of hibernation in which we may either wake up from it and find the era of our own dinosaurs of fear has folded its sad and gloomy chapter or at worst may have installed its kingdom of skulls and blood even deeper and hence, we may conclude that this relative time of ours on earth is definitely over and we may declare our own South Sudanese dinosaurs of fear the winners just like Omer Al Bashier over the innocent Sudanese.

Who may have expected that the good South Sudan that we have known, lived in it, enjoyed our mud games and the songs of the innocent birds, the greens of the land and of course the uniqueness of its good people and in a time where our only weapons were spears and steaks aimed mostly on hunting deer and the fresh fish on those Waats*(pools) of ours. Who may have expected that this land will breed the dinosaurs of fear at a time we were expecting to relax and have a break from the lengthy journey of war after war, refuge after refuge?

Funny isn't it that not long ago we were talking about Omer Al-Bashier annexing Abyei, Kosti and Heglig towns from South to North but now we are cheaply spilling our own blood on who own Malakal, Pajut, Pigi and Akobo. Funny isn't it that in just a while ago we were talking about South Sudanese being given the bones out of the fat meat of Sudan and that the North was the sure evil of all evils. How did the clock turned around in the opposite direction and heaven upside down in a matter of split second? What is playing with our minds, souls, and hearts?

Why would we continue to dream in a land of fear and where the precious life hangs between uncertainty and the mercy of our own dinosaurs of fears? Why would we continue to dream in a land of fear and hatred where dreams are cut short, destroyed and thrown into the unknown? Dreams of these innocents' kids of having a play, a candy, a pen, and a notebook and to wake up in early mornings when the cock crows, hurrying to schools and learn a thing or two. Dreams of these kids to be doctors, lawyers, and presidents. Dreams of these young girls to be beauty queens, brides, nurses and angels. Dreams of a nation to have peace, life, and happiness. Why would we continue to dreams in a land of fear?

I wish our leaders have some good dreams for this country, dreams to see Juba lighten up like New York, dreams of high rises in Juba like Dubai. Dreams of great hospitals, paved roads and highways, dream of "Made in South Sudan". I wish our leaders have dreams of having prestigious Universities like MIT, Harvard and Stanford, dreams of seeing their people live longer, live happier, live securer and until they can dream and have dreams for us and the country, we the people will have to enter into a long hibernation and suspends our dreams until further notice. Wake me up when it happens.

May 24, 2016
In a Nutshell

The controversy over Mr. Machar praying at Emmanuel Jieng Church is a reminder to us of who we are and whether we would be a stable and developed, united and prosperous nation in the long run. Even though I think the move from Mr. Machar and as usual, has a well and good intents however, I think it is hasty, risky and untimely and should be done in an organized manner that is part of overall nation reconciliation and healing campaign and not as an individual move simply because the mood in Juba and around the country is still very much in upheaval state and Mr. Machar should wait until it normalizes and become less hostile.

As a nation of South Sudan, we either have to choose to reconcile and move on together, build a place for us among the civilized and developed nations of the world and a better future for our children or at worse choose to be held standstill or going backward, hostages by our past grudges and the bias of envy, pry and vengeance. Wisdom is, let us choose to move on and build a better reality, a better country and a great nation and the world history is our redeemer as it show us that none of today great nations on earth such as the American, the European and the South African have had the same troubled past like ours that ranges from long and bloody civil wars, racism, economic depression and acute social woes that almost brought them crumbling into pieces nevertheless, they came out stronger, wiser, and united than ever and hence learning from such experiences, decided to set themselves on a path that is different from the sad past, a path of reconciliation, healing, unity and collective purpose.

The reality is, the greater Bor community which dominate the said church, have ever since the first Mr. Machar apology of the 1991 Bor massacres been divided over of whether to accept and forgive Mr. Machar and with part of the Greater Bor community has shown readiness to reconcile with him and the Nuer community at large leaving behind the awful past grudges, envy and vengeance and choosing instead, the unity, peace for the nation and better future for the generations to come and not only that but some went to become the best and powerful allies of Mr. Machar in his quest for change and reforms in the country. Unfortunately, some of the greater Bor has never and would never accept Mr. Machar bid for reconciliation and will never forgive him no matter how many apologies he echoed to the said community and hence has chosen to endlessly fight the man in every way possible, politically or militarily and as long as he is alive and has a political present in the country. Those who are out of the greater Bor community are also manipulating the 1991 tragedy for political objectives that range from dividing the greater Upper Nile region and setting apart the two larger communities of South Sudan, the Dinka and Nuer for cheap personal and tribal political gains.

While we deeply understand the magnitudes of the loss of the families of the victims of the 1991 Bor Massacres just like the same of 2013 Nuer Juba massacres or any of the bloody ethnic based massacres committed in the land of South Sudan, we believe that the future of the country can't let be a prisoner of the sad past and as a nation we must choose to reconcile and move on for our own good. Revenge and counter revenge is an endless bloody cycle that never ends with a lose-win tribal revenges but a win-win reconciliation, healing and peaceful co-existence between the concerned tribes and as a nation at large. However, the problem with reconciliation and healing in South Sudan is that it is not done in the way that could give the victims' families and relatives the true redemption, satisfaction and healing in order for them to forgive and move on with the alleged perpetrators.

Another aspect making the attempt for healing and reconciliation worthless is the politics of interests in which some of these so-called politicians of ours see their stay in power very much linked or connected in a way or another on keeping the tribal divide and past grudges alive and aflame, keeping them to fuel their political substance and reign and as long as those kind of politicians are around, it is going to be a hit on the rock for South Sudanese to come together. Healing and reconciliation is crucial for this country and nation to move on, it bring us together as a nation in a healthy front that will build South Sudan of the future, South Sudan the great, the peaceful and the prosperous as we may envision it.

May 26, 2016
In a Nutshell

Competition is the magic of private sector, it encourages businesses to compete within the ethical and legal settings to provide better services and products, encourage innovation and creativity and since each business is on offensive to enhance its competitive advantage, the reality is that private sector is the essence of a sustainable economy. if we assume that it is only one company that's in monopoly of market whether in service or production area, that company without a good rival or competitor in the said business won't have the needed reasons why it should perform better, provide quality products or services and accordingly, the prices of its services/products could be a skyrocket high.

Politically and in South Sudan, this is the case of having a one party, the ruling SPLM, dominating the political power and space for the last 35 years without a significant political rival rather than its own internal-conflicts born factions and militias who are no better than their own mainstream mother. The lack of viable political rival, strong, in both substance and leadership to the SPLM has made the later dysfunctional and ineffective in terms of performance and political program, lazy and sleeping at that power seat without a threat of significant political competitor. In a political market where the SPLM found itself the only sole player, it has forgotten the very good objectives it was founded for and in fact turned against them.

If there was a good political competitor who can take the advantage and use the shortcomings of SPLM, its poor performance in service delivery, poor leadership and management of nation-state affairs and its tribal approach rather than a national approach we could have seen a paradigm shift in both public opinion and the political message opting for better alternatives. Operating on the SPLM/A's liberation legacy and historical role without timely sustainable transformation agenda that's translating the liberation into reality has become an empty song without a meaning. The reality is, the South Sudanese people are poorer than when they weren't "liberated" and being killed, jailed and tortured than when they weren't "independent". Hunger, insecurity is prevalent and forcing the ordinary South Sudanese to pack in thousands heading to the Sudan, once the hell and evil like no other, unfortunately, they may have discovered a hell and evil here that have vindicated the former Sudan.

The point is, we need another strong party in South Sudan political market that should operate parallel and opposite in direction "when necessary" to the "lost" SPLM. A party that will be the alternative good leadership and that will outperform the " Dysfunctional " SPLM and with a culture of transparency and accountability that is better than the "Corrupted' SPLM and with a national inclusive program that is for all South Sudan that is better than the program of 'Tribalist" SPLM and I can assure you when such a party emerges and with all the indicators pointing to the fact that it is pulling the carpet of power from the "Sleeping" SPLM, the later will either have to re-invent itself on good basis in order to survive in the political market of South Sudan or vanish to the world of political extinction. Well, the question of course is who have the courage and the needed leadership assets to initiate and form such a party of challenge.

May 27, 2016
In a Nutshell

It is clear that the Transitional Government of National Unity (TGoNU) will be another venue for lengthy negotiations and wrangling over the pending issues of disagreement between the peace and war partners now the government partners. Such a trend will rob the TGoNU from its expected priorities of recovery and healing and would instead divert its focus to by-issues and endless political wrangling of who should win in what rather than agreeing on a minimum common ground of priorities that are needed to rescue the country from economic collapse and possibility of return to war.

The 28 states row is a real threat to peace in its entirety and it would require a political wet and flexibility from both of us, leadership and people of South Sudan, handling it carefully and without rush or ego-centric mentality. We must all understand how would president Kiir feel about reversing his 36/2015 decree that brought to life the controversial 28 states. He definitely knows that the reversal would be beginning of the real retreat of his unpopular decrees and policies and much more to his political career. He knows this would mean a grand political defeat and would divide his own camp while at same time it would be a huge political gains to the SPLM/A-IO and allies and accordingly, I believe Kiir would neither abolish his 28 states decree in its wholeness rather than choose a compromise with the various stakeholders in regard to issues of disputes within the 28 states.

News and rumors has it that a committee has been formed to work on boundaries of those 28 states and later come with recommendations after its investigations and findings. Well, haven't seen the composition of such a committee if there one for sure, neither its members and who is who or whether it has a balanced, inclusive and national representation particularly of those whose lands are claimed to have been annexed neither whether this committee does include the experts of history, map, geography of South Sudan and which the investigations and findings and recommendations should be based. Well, such a task is truly difficult, costly and time consuming than the decree of 28 states itself and neither have we known that the committee's findings and recommendation will be equally welcomed, accepted and will be abided with by the concerned communities.

The reality is, the 28 states decree was one of series of techniques and policies meant for Mr. Kiir survival during the war with his arch rival Dr. Riek Machar and the logic should dictate him reversing them as the threat and war are almost over and with Dr. Machar now a fundamental part of his government and who in his part sidelined his 21 states proposal. However, let's note that the 10 states are not also just and fair in their representation and the 28 states came with some positive solutions to some of the 10 states such as the then troubled Jonglei and Lakes states and I doubt whether the people within these states would be ready to roll back to the same miserable state of the past.

All in all, for the TGoNU not to be held hostage by the 28 states or the SPLA-IO cantonment issues in both Bar Al-Gazal and Equatoria region and the subsequent lengthy negotiations and which may take time and end in limbo, president Kiir must again take some courageous steps to end the row over those issues and pave the way for the real implementation of peace agreement. South Sudan is here to stay and any president can come and go and whether 10 or 28 states or even 50, it is the same South Sudan land and is not going anywhere.

June 3, 2016
In a Nutshell

While the whole country focus is being confined on things that don't matter, the bones and not the fat meat, it seems the resource-rich South Sudan may find its way to a healthy country and society with the next generations and not the current one, well, at least if the later haven't checkmated all the future opportunities to them (the future generations). Too late to educate or undo the biased concepts of this generation and hence one expectation is that the impact and the consequences of ignorance can't be escaped nor avoided and that we are destined for a lifetime where tribalism, poverty, and insecurity for the next 50 years is a sure reality.

As an engineer or a leader, to be wrong from start is a sure disaster to the building or the nation you are trying to build respectively because what happens next and above the wrong foundation is either both costly or endlessly problematic and it could be too late either to trace it back that easily to the source because part of it may have already got lost in translation and probably it could be mistaken to a different reasoning and not rightly to the underneath wrong foundation. As we may freshly remember how our own recent crisis that has went through various realms of confusion, from a one political party disagreement to tribal war to either God's curse or a prophet prophecies and other interpretations, well, that isn't a surprise either since most of the social or political problems don't stay at the point of origin but they get complicated with time, get twisted, manipulated and in that course, they breed more complicated problems than the source problem itself.

Given Sudan as example, it been 65 years since its independence but the country never witnessed a day without a war with itself, not with an external enemy but with itself, from the days it was still a united country until today even when the separation of South was thought to be the right recipe for both north and south to live peacefully and in stability thereafter but this turned not to be the case as it is clearly reflected in the current miserable state of affairs of both South and North of Sudan who currently are in much socio-economic and political troubles than ever. 65 years is never quite a short time, not if Sudan was founded right from start on sound bases, given its resources, no reason why it could just be rich and well developed just like Gulf countries and others who got their independence at 50s and 60s. Similarly, South Sudan discourse and future is no different and with the current wrong from start approach, in 65 years later, the country shall find itself in the same spot as Sudan or worst if a U-turn is not made to what is right.

Right from start, if our aim is to be a nation and a country where the sole objective is for every law abiding citizen to have a dignified life, balanced between the duties and rights, we could been in agreement to start with the right programs-both short and long-term that would transform us to such a great destination and noble objective, such as massive education programs or call it a revolution with clear set objectives and goals, adequate re-engineering of our social norms and values right after the independence, a one that leaves the constructive ones and eliminates the biased and destructive ones, tribalism could have been channeled as cultural face of South Sudan but not necessarily its political system, we could have set ourselves distinctively apart from the influence of our neighbors, corruption at its both types could have been minimized and the new wave of brutal crimes could have been avoided and those who have been living in South Sudan before the war or the independence may catch what I mean about South Sudan that we cherished and dream to bring back.

Well, our problems are not people based rather than leadership based, it is the leadership that haven't had a vision right from start that's based on a nation of South Sudan but instead we had a divisive one based on tribes and tribal manipulation. This is because our leaders have chosen power over country and nation; they needed tribalism as a way for power and a substance to feeds their stay on it.

The questions are; where do we go from here? Who is leading the way, who cares about us, who is directing us to a better future, who is protecting and securing the future of this nation and country? A nation without a caring and responsible leaders is an orphaned nation, and as you see the insecurity is killing us but we have no one to turn to, the hunger is finishing us but no one care, the future is being destroyed, represented in these thousands of malnourished children, kids without schools for 3 years, the sick are dying with the curable diseases, our unemployed and frustrated youth turned to gangs and crime but no one care but you won't miss a day without hearing your Excellency and Honorable and wonders for what is the excellence and honor while the constituents are dying at their own watch.

June 5, 2016
In a Nutshell

Looking like the TGoNU will be a big and confused government and here are the reasons, we have too many partners that are making sure they are represented and in that context there will be a lot of confusion and overlap in defining job descriptions, duties, and responsibilities and with much of these constitutional holders being there for just the title and salary.

Well, peace must be bought and it seems this is the huge

price of the expensive peace that is highly needed to return our country back from the bloody war, 19 advisors to the presidency will make your mind wonders why is that and what they are for, advising the presidency on what? Well, as I mentioned above, the TGoNU is a representative government more than it is a limited and task-specific government and this is due to the fact that the two TGoNU partners must satisfy their vast political supporters who were left out in the TGoNU ministers reshuffle and hence come with this horrible idea of accommodating them as advisors, Gen. Kiir started it, with huge 10 advisors from his own party and then the SPLM-IO and the rest objected and demanded either the decree be revoked or matched by a quota from their own parties.

Hence comes the 19 advisors who are as well constitutional holders with privileges and salaries same as national ministers and accordingly we have a government of 3 members of the presidency, of nearly 45 national ministers, 28 governors, 28 deputy governors, more than 140 states ministers leave alone the 1000s of top generals in the police and the army, directors and their deputies in all departments of the government. This wouldn't be a problem if we have the financial resources to give any one a job to quell the tendencies for troubles and to silence the guns even though the idea in its entirety is wrong and a total waste of resources but it seems it is the price of buying the expensive peace at least for now.

However, this huge bargain for peace comes with some logical questions that shouldn't be ignored such as; does the government or the country have the money for all that? Was there any coordination between the fiscal budget of years 2016-2017 and government spending, Tax revenues, production revenues or does the government has any cash reserve or other clear known funding entities? The oil sector is still under-performing and the efforts for repairing the damage caused by war to its refineries and production capacity may take at least 6 months to 1 year before it come back to full health and production, well, if by that time, the oil markets are not going to be in the same struggle as now.

The country needs more financial resources to solve its humanitarian problems caused by the recent war, resettling our millions of refugees from neighboring countries and the IDPs in the UN compounds as well as for funding its healing and reconciliation campaign, boost its fragile security to encourage the return of those refugees and IDPs alike as well as international investors, trade and commerce between its various states and along its neighboring borders and which may accelerate the bid for economic recovery.

All in all, the presidency is moving quite well on bringing the country back to peace and stability reflected by the recent actions which are more positive and encouraging than ever. Well, we wish they continue with the same cohesion and collective spirit in solving the problems of the nation, leading collectively as a one entity and not as three conflicting heads. Let us hope for the best.

June 6, 2016
In a Nutshell

Security must improve for everything else to improve in South Sudan, no one is going to invest his/her hard-earned money in a country with a fragile security shield, where people are being killed, robbed and properties looted in a daylight and where the goods and the people can't move freely between the various states of South Sudan and from South Sudan to its many neighbors and vice versa.

The war has trashed South Sudan image in a great deal and it may need double efforts just to reclaim the confidence of the world represented by the potential investors, funding and financial institutions. An economic boom does not just happen out of the blue, it has its first prerequisites, apart from adequate economic planning, there is a need for a conducive environment, a comprehensive and professional security plan with clear objectives and goals aimed at securing people and not terrorizing them and that encourage the confidence in government institutions and the system, that create an atmosphere where people securely trade and perform the sales and purchasing activities. It is from all these businesses activities the government generates its revenues through taxation and others services and hence the government should be the first entity that is keen to protect people and their businesses and to make sure the security situation is economically encouraging and viable. Insecurity of course will send the potential investors to somewhere else that is relatively secure and economically stable.

Maybe it is the oil that has given us this lazy trend of having money without knowing that they are labored and earned through hard work and managed in a way that must add value. Khartoum has explored the oil, put in place all the oil production installations and Juba has found everything operating well and sound after the independence and hence Juba has no feeling that these oil industry was built through years of hard work and patience and accordingly its money must be managed wisely, invested efficiently and that someday this oil may stop for this reason or that. I think we need planning of what we want to become as a nation, how we can make ourselves better in all aspects and I think we have the minds that can thinks, the educated that can manifest those plans into reality.

This bring us to wonders whether Juba does labor ideas when it comes to governance and administration of the nation affairs, ideas for improving the nation standards of living, ideas for inclusive development of the country, Ideas like what do to light up the whole South Sudan, to provide clean waters, to connect South Sudan all states through paved roads, ideas to make every citizen secure and to boost trade between various states, to build Juba as international capital for trade and investment, Ideas to melt these shattered tribes of ours into one nation and not the other way around. Well, if we cease to think for ourselves and invent ways that improves our lives and the future generation then we definitely are victims of someone else who may think for us in a way that doesn't work for us.

Security doesn't mean securing only the president and the elite in the government and leaving the rest of the country vulnerable to the hyenas of the unknown gunmen of all sorts to do whatever they want with it. The people of South Sudan need security and the national intelligence and security constitutional job are to do just that and not only to secure the elite and themselves. Security is the backbone of the economy just as people, you got to have a healthy, secure and free people that can think without fears, live and works without being terrorized by phenomenon of the unknown gunmen. People can't dream and thinks freely when it is only fears is engulfing them, when they know their dreams are worthless and will be cut short.

There is a need for professionalism in security sector because now it is being misused and the powers there are being abused, people are being harassed, jailed, kidnapped, tortured and killed at worst for personal and tribal reasons and the national security agency has lost its mandate and the reasons behind its establishment. There is a need for strict laws and regulations in security sector, and the security personnel are not above the law neither they are judges to end people lives, jail and detain people as they wish, there must be a legal due process and where it should end with a fair trial, fair defense lawyers and fair sentence by a judge. South Sudan security just remind us of the movie of Idi Amin Dada of Uganda or the SSS of Germany's Hitler and the question is who is going to live in such a country leave alone to go and invest his hard-earn money? If you need a better economy and a better country, the security sector reform is a serious matter and it must be tackled.

June 9, 2016
In a Nutshell

Absolutely there is a need for justice and accountability for the crimes committed during 2013-2016 war and still being committed even today at some parts of Equatoria region and other parts of South Sudan However, it is ironic to believe that this justice and accountability for these horrible crimes will be done and ensured by the same people who committed them. The International community has no clue what it is talking about neither it will invade South Sudan to capture Kiir or Machar or all the warlords here that 90% of them are the ministers in TGoNU. Unless Kiir and Machar can disown their factions and commanders who were fighting for them and apparently engaged in those horrible atrocities, well not likely because this move has its consequences to the two leaders and they are fully aware of it and hence would rather unite their front and oppose the international community instead of being the victims of such approach.

Well, here are possible two scenarios that are likely to be the best options for ensuring accountability for the victims and punishment for alleged perpetrators; if it is about peace and accountability the best scenario is an accountability in the form of compensation and reconciliation that the international community would help to finance and facilitate its process of healing and reconciliation. If it is about punishment for the alleged perpetrators and accountability for the victims, then the other unlikely scenario is for Kiir and Machar to resign and a new government should take over and ensure the establishment of trials of both Kiir and Machar and their commanders and which is far from happening. The South Africa Truth, healing and reconciliation model might not work fully in South Sudan given the differences in both actors and circumstances. The Apartheid regime was no longer a government when those trials or the truth and reconciliation process was taking place but a new government with the help of international community was the one conducting the process.

People went to the bush to fight Kiir for the Juba massacres of 2013, however the whole campaign of Kiir must go crumbled like no other and Kiir couldn't be removed and in which if it happens, the new government could try and punish Kiir and his associates in the crimes of 2013-2016 but this isn't the case now, Kiir and his all men of war are all here, leading the TGoNU. Let us not forget that we haven't removed Kiir but instead we came and begged Kiir for peace and to allow us to come to Juba until now the SPLM/A-IO is a part of TGoNU in which Kiir is still the head. Now the international community is telling Kiir to try and punish himself and not only that but the approach is unified to include Machar the assumed victim with Kiir the alleged perpetrator of the crimes, this approach is risky because it will blow-off all the peace efforts being waged at the movement and may led to differences and confrontations the international community won't be able to contain and may result in new victims and atrocities of wide scale far brutal than the ones we are trying to account for.

South Sudan is the victim and the perpetrator here, in a war of its own and regardless whether there are regional or international invisible hands that has ignited this war, pitting the two largest communities against themselves and any idiot in politics may be aware of the fact that the road to destruction or greatness of South Sudan come through the simple philosophy of putting the Dinka and Nuer against each or with each other's, respectively. The state of South Sudan must do its own reconciliation its own way, bring it people together, in a successive peaceful process aimed to heal the wounds of the bloody war, hatred of the divisive tribalism and politics.

A national prayer every month, where the diverse people of South Sudan come all together, every month, pray, sing and have time together in reconciliation and the forgiving bid, will help bring our people together and the media, private and public shepherded by SSBC in particular has a crucial role in the healing and reconciliation process and hence a new staff with a peaceful and national approach may be put in charge to help create a new peaceful public opinion and environment. The international community can help finance such a process and not necessarily ties their money with their own approach that might not work in South Sudan.

June 11, 2016
In a Nutshell

Almost laughed my heart out when I learned today that some members of the SPLM/A-IO decided to defect to the side of Kiir and that the defection technique is still active and being used to beg for jobs back and forth from the then warring factions turned partners in the current Transitional Government of National Unity (TGoNU) even for some insignificant people whose defection have no damage or weight whatsoever on their former movement in which they have defected from. Ironically enough, the state-run SSBC has decided to be part of these damaging efforts from anti-peace forces, well, this has to stop because they are clear hostile activities against the SPLM/A-IO and which is a clear breach of ARCSS provisions which clearly call for prohibition of hostile media and propaganda so an atmosphere of peace, healing and reconciliation can be realized instead.

But it seems our opportunists are in a different realm and shamelessly collaborating behind the scene with the anti-peace forces and which give them false and empty promises of employment and promotion in return for defection and who knows maybe some cash too if the kings of corruption in Juba still have some money in their own local and foreign banks. Probably the defection propaganda and the published article in New York Times (NYT) are all but coordinated conspiracy planned and executed by the same anti-piece group who are trying to undermine the current peace efforts, planting new obstacles and poisoning the political environment in a wish for new troubles and conflicts. But the question of course is, if we assumed that Kiir and base are keen in their partnership with SPLM/A-IO to position the country into the path of peace and recovery then why they are letting such spoilers to conspire in an attempt to prevent and spoil the country path back to recovery and normalcy, well, unless Kiir and base are in a new bid for troubles and war, these hostile moves against the SPLM/A –IO should have stopped from the day Dr. Machar returned to Juba.

Undoubtedly, there are some people within the system that have committed themselves to never rest until they failed the peace process and until they bring the two partners in TGoNU into a new reality of political or at worse military confrontations and hostilities and it is in the interest of peace and that of the country to not let such elements to succeeds. President Kiir has a role and power to either replace or direct such spoilers to stop this kind of damaging activities and particularly in a volatile environment as of Juba's. Otherwise, these spoilers are not alone and they are just acting on behalf of Kiir and base.

Well, my fears are that amidst the current political confusion and rivalry, the anti-peace elements may succeed one day to set the whole situation on fire. These anti-peace elements are smart and knew where and when to confuse the public opinion and exploit most of the differences between the partners of peace agreement as it is sustained by what was happening in Juba before December 2013 as the news of coup after coup were being circulated and disseminated between time and then until the former regime approved and believed in one of them, the one that broke the Camel's back on December15th, 2013.

All in all, there is good trend amidst the lies of liars and the conspiracies of the conspirators and it is that the South Sudanese people regardless of their political differences and tribal affiliations are starting to form a unified front against what is false and what is irrational and I realized that there are a good number of people now who are criticizing misleading leaders from their own tribes and praising good leaders from different tribes. This is a great development because what has destroyed South Sudan is that people most often sides with what is wrong because it is coming from one of their own and rejecting the truth because its source is from the opposite tribe, such an approach has created a country that is built on false rather than the truth until we have reached to the middle of nowhere.

June 14, 2016
In a Nutshell

Well, I wish the corruption case of the 16 officials of president's office sentenced today to life in prison will not be like the case of those 75 officials or the $4 billion that has ended miserably. The 16 officials aren't just going to be just quiet, so expect their reactions or that of their associates. Sometimes I wish I can understand how things in president Kiir's office really works, whether he is in charge and know whatever is taking place in his office or whether he is just an innocent man being manipulated by greedy hyenas around him whom he trusted with everything and unfortunately they turned against him, forging the president seal and signature to embezzle millions of public money or whether it is just a temporary movie aimed at diverting our wondering minds. But the president office case wasn't the first and the course of corruption in South Sudan haven't started with it and as we remember there are cases of corruption with magnitude bigger than president's office case albeit the later was taken seriously by the president and landed its dependents a life in prison sentence.

Well, as usual, we thought the dependents in this case, will go free and get away with their crimes as that of Dura $4 billion case but to our surprise it didn't and maybe it is due to two possibilities in regard to the unexpected sentence in this particular case of corruption; either the president has initiated a new era of fight against all types of graft that has destroyed our nation for the last 11 years since 2005 or this trial and sentence could be just a drama intended to mislead the public and international community in an attempt to regain public trust and foreign investors respectively.

Some are arguing that how come now President Kiir could distinguish himself from his government, as the head of the government, a corrupt government since 2005. Is it the bitter realization that things have reached a dead-end and that the country has totally bankrupted as a result of public money being laundered and embezzled in millions where they have ended without a trace in foreign countries? Isn't too late to wash oneself after reaching to the very depth of muddy valley with the same muddy waters while the whole country has a very strong conviction now that Mr. president if not the head of the corruption himself then he has been tolerating and harboring corruption and not only that some go to an extent of being hopeless in the fight against corruption and that it will never end because the leadership, with the president included, is deep in it.

But today one would wonders if president Kiir is a corrupt then how could a corrupt leader let his corrupt associates be tried publicly and sentenced to life in prison without the fear that these associates may confess and spill the beans about his role in such corruption activities and schemes? I know some of us don't believe that this drama is truly real and authentic rather than an act meant to mislead the public and that sooner or later, all these men sentenced today to life in prison will definitely go free as they have the right to appeal the sentence anytime. Well, here how it will go, if it is just a drama that has no truth in it, then expect all the men to be free sooner or later. However, if the men are set to rot in prisons for life, then we have a job to do, vindicating president Kiir from all the false accusations that we have been labeling him since the start of corruption in 2005.

President Kiir could be a clean man only that he has fallen a victim of circle of greedy hyenas who has surrounded him in every corner and direction, financially as well as in public policy and with corruption booming at financial institutions and public money being embezzled in millions, the public policy was diverted to sustain the corruption line and as a one tribe system while it has nothing to do with that in fact with such a claim a but a one that is serving the interests of the corrupted few. President Kiir could be just a victim of smart mafia around him as the case of corruption in the president office indicates as well as the fabricated coup of 2013 otherwise, his jailed associates and soon to be fired subordinates will have to tell us the real Kiir that we may not know. This or that, time will tell.

June 17, 2016
In a Nutshell

While efforts are being made to quell the fire of 2013 war, it seems new rebellions are surfacing in many different corners of the troubled South Sudan and the recent Raja and Keji fights are clear indicators of such a claim. Contrary to the sayings of SPLA-IG chief of staff, Paul Malong that "there is smoke without fire in South Sudan" these incidents seem to be not falling in his poor categorization and instead strongly emphasize that there is no smoke without fire in South Sudan and these armed men who overrun the capital of the newly created Lol state or those who are involved in Keji incident are neither SPLA-IO nor just armed bandits who are simply returning home after being chased away by Malong's SPLA as Mr. Lul Ruai Koang has claimed.

These are armed movements in the making and for reasons known to their members and leadership and which mostly I believe it is connected to the 28 states new borders that some said to have annexed minorities tribes' lands or has weaken some minorities tribes by distributing them in powerless tiny groups within majority dominant tribes in an attempt to erase their existence gradually and then have the land. These policies of land grabbing can't ever create a peaceful, united South Sudan and no matter what, when it comes to the land issues, no matter how big or small are the people whose land is being occupied by force; the resistance and the fight to win back one's land will always be constant and active.

Ironically enough, these new armed movements are starting from the Bar Al-Gazel and Equatoria regions, two of the three major regions of South Sudan geopolitical division and which were largely less affected by the conflict of 2013 and its subsequent bloody war in which the third major region, the greater Upper Nile region, was its center of the three years' bloody war and field of its heinous atrocities. Now while the Upper Nile region is yearning for the return of peace and security it seems the two regions are about to kick start their own rebellions. Well, the irony of the matter is the call by the SPLA's Malong Spokesman, Lul Ruai Kong that the SPLA-IO must fight alongside the SPLA-IG in its new fight against the emerging new armed movements.

Such a malicious call is of two folds, with the first being to test the SPLM/A-IO whether it is part of the new armed movements or working with them behind the scene, the second aspect is to drag the SPLM/A –IO into a fight against those who are opposing the 28 states and in which the SPLM/A-IO is the vocal ad major opponent and warned of its implications. If the SPLM/A-IO opted for rejection, then SPLM/A-IG has its already made accusations to the former by being part or the driver of the new armed movement and if the SPLM/A-IO decided to participate in the war against the new armed movement then this its end of what it been calling for and particularly the opposition to 28 states.

Well, I think the SPLM/A-IO will not fall into that trap

rather than pursue a middle ground to be a deal maker between itself, the new armed movements and the Kiir's 28 states establishment (JCE and others). However, don't forget that this is another political boiling point in which new political realities may emerge and as long as the 28 states decree is here, the political hunt and conspiracies are going to be the new politics of the day and as far as this 28 states is concerned this could be a new coordinated front for another long war against the TGoNU or until the TGoNU itself is pitted against itself.

Well, may God grant mercy on the innocent lives that are perishing as a result of such controversial policies and politics of our leaders in Juba and which became the source of death everywhere in this country and as we sadly and continuously losing a good number of young people in much senseless violence as a reason of failed politics and poor decision-making.

June 21, 2016
In a Nutshell

Unless you are new to the realm of African political mindset, nothing should make you believe that the more the international community exercised more economic sanctions or financial assistance denial, the more likely the African dictators will succumb to their end or at least they would lower their tight grip on power or open up for reforms and restructuring of their dysfunctional institutions and systems. Such perception has been proven wrong in many similar situations in Africa and has shown the contrary instead of what was expected where the only people who are really being punished are the ordinary citizens and not the dictators and their entourages who has thrived even more and stayed in power even longer.

Well, this is because the ruling elite has amassed huge

financial assets through the many years of their stay in power and by various corruption means and methods and hence they are far from being affected by the impact of financial and economic sanctions neither they have a reputation that is left and that they do care about, since they have done all the forbidden and hence they are even ready to plunge the country and the nation into sure collapse if they sense their end is imminent. To sum it up, the international community in its drive to see some tangible change and reforms through the pressure and financial assistance card may be hurting the people of South Sudan and the peace process instead because I don't see the ruling elite as giving up power whatsoever unless they got evicted by force, something I doubt the international community can even think about.

Blocking all the gates to all better alternatives, Mr. Salva is here to stay despite that all indicators are pointing to what we have predicted couple months ago when the local currency was floated against the dollar that the suffering of South Sudanese people will double and that the country will find itself ultimately bankrupted. However, a different scenario maybe the case as many are pointing out that the Juba ruling elite upon the coming of the SPLM/A-IO, have emptied the banks and government's various departments from any financial resources and transferred them into their own personal accounts in anticipation of the expected international community financial assistance for the peace implementation, well, that didn't happens as they have wished and accordingly we have a bankrupted government and country now but make no mistake about it, the ruling elite are even richer and stronger.

As each one of us may remember, South Sudan has a long story with the help and assistance from the International community since it was at war with the North and throughout the 23+ years of liberation struggle, it has been a dependent child of the international community and which believed like anyone else in the just cause of the Sudanese people and until we have got our independence 5 years ago. But what happen after the independence is our own faults, the peak of greed, mismanagement and poor leadership in a way that has astonished the whole world and will make the international community thinks twice and reluctant in helping us once more time.

Should we blame the international community after all it have done to us? Should we continuously be dependent to the help of the international community? What will be the meaning of the independence? What do we think about the consequences when we mismanage our own affairs, rob our own country and send its financial assets to live lavishly in foreign countries? Should we blame someone else for our own failed policies and decision-making apparatus? You don't destroy your country or mismanage your nation's affairs at will and then look for help from the international community and the ironic part of it is that, the ruling elite are in constant state of denial nor showing any sign of guilt or any need for redemption but instead they are still affirming strongly that all their actions and decisions are right and sound even thus they are seeing the sure drastic outcomes.

All in all, and not long ago, when have started opposing the wrong policies and inefficient plans of the ruling elite in Juba because we knew they are leading to this dead end. However, the ruling elite were quick to unleash its own defensive propaganda and pretext crying out loud that our constructive criticism is because it is a government of this tribe and an opposition of that tribe and that because the president hail from this region and the opposition leader is from that region and so and so but by now, the suffering people of South Sudan and regardless of their different tribes and regions are the one paying the heavy price of the ruling elite's failed policies and decisions, well, time still will unveil more.

June 26, 2016
In a Nutshell

Kiir's Kalashnikov AK 47 is traveling real fast, gunning down everyone that is saying no to his domination, marginalization policies and decrees, yesterday it was the Nuer in Bentiu, Nasir and Ayod, next was the Murle in Pibor and the Choli in Malakal to Mundri in Equatoria and Dinka in Tonj until it reached Wau today, slaughtering the innocent Frertit, Jur and the rest of those peaceful minorities tribes that we hardly hear about in South Sudan constant political chaos and wrangling. When Kiir send his tribal Army to crush the so-called armed youth or groups, you know it is the innocent civilians being massacred, their properties being looted and destroyed, you know that it is either a tribal or clannish revenge that is taking place and people will be kill because they are from the suspected and target tribe or clan and not because of anything else, the neutrality and nationalism of Kiir's army is a gone case long time ago.

Maybe a tribal president this time and a tribal army at another but to have them both at the same time then that's the hellish nightmare of those being ruled and this is the miserable state of affairs of the people of South Sudan being ruled by tribal president Salva Kiir and his tribal army the SPLA-Malong and if your life is spared by one, it will be ended by the other and like that the South Sudanese people have fought and endured the 50 years of bitter struggle against the domination of the North Sudan just to found themselves in a Kiir Kuethpiny's domination, harsher than the one we thought before as the hell on all the earth.

Kiir Kuethpiny is far from being a national leader for all South Sudan neither his army can go for a national army of the country, they both lost this virtue from the day of Juba massacre, when he and his tribal army deliberately targeted one ethnic group the Nuer under the pretext of Riek Machar's fabricated coup and then the Nuer resisted a three year of being cornered, selected to be a target of everyone in South Sudan, fighting against all including Uganda. Everyone was thinking and believing it is a Nuer problem, their greed for power, their love for troubles and violence and all the sort of lies and propaganda. Well, the Nuer in a rare resilience took it all upon themselves, fought Kiir Kuethpiny and his tribal army, his Sudanese mercenaries, and the Museveni hired-to-kill army for a bloody three years of huge sacrifices.

The Nuer prevailed and the big lie of the coup and the well woven fabricated defamation and propaganda all faltered like no other and as we have said it from the very inception of this crisis that the Kiir leadership has failed and failed miserably in leading the nation-state building and this never about Nuer or Dinka nor about Riek Machar but that Kiir has no such a thing as leadership skills when it comes to leading a diverse nation such as South Sudanese. Kiir could be a good soldier, a skilled intelligence officer who might be good at conspiracy theories, spying and cold blood killings but when it comes to leading a nation and country, I must be honest and as evidenced by his 11 years' rule, he doesn't have it.

Kiir's decision-making system has been disastrous and one of the main contributing factor in South Sudan's problems since the drastic removal of the national government cabinet in 2013 and which triggered the 2013 political turmoil and its subsequent Juba massacre, then the 28 states decree which immediately started the bloody tribal conflicts on land and territories and which has started from his hometown Warrup with over 90 casualties and then the Malakal massacre and now the Wau massacre with both casualties estimated at no less than 100. Kiir also has been removing and arresting states' governors unconstitutionally and like he is removing his gatekeepers with no the slightest regards or consideration to the consequences or the implications of such drastic decisions and decrees at either state security or national security level and the case of W. Equatoria governor Bakasoro and Wau governor are good examples.

You could lead a liberation war or an army to a battle successfully but this doesn't give you the needed brains and the guts of being a president. However, history has also given many examples of soldiers who were also great politicians and constructive leaders but honestly Kiir is not one of them. Being a president of a country is completely a different thing you need to have a different vision, sound socio-economic and political policies, you have to be the sun for all your people irrespective of their differences, political colors or ethnicity, the father of all your children, the leader of all your tribes, you have to be the one that unites, that redeem, that reconcile, the peace's keeper and fixer of the problems. Alas, our president has been the contrary in every aspect and sometimes one feel sorry whether the man has destroyed himself at will or has been destroyed by his inner circle of all interests' groups, it is a very sad mystery. Mr. Kiir could have resigned gracefully with a great legacy he earned well by being one of the co-founders of the SPLM/A and the first president of an independent South Sudan and he could have ushered the nascent country to a bright path in democracy, nationalism, and unity but that wasn't the case, instead he decided to hold his tight grip on power, delivering nothing but destroying himself, his country and his nation.

Now the failure of president Kiir is strongly evident in

every aspect, the country has collapsed in every way, bankrupted economically, destroyed socially and politically divided, the nation is starving, largely insecure and tribally divided than ever, the local currency pound now equal $50 compared to $2 three years ago when we just got our independence, people around the country have not been paid for the last 4 to 6 months. Ironically enough, president Kiir has the courage and the guts to start new conflicts and bloodshed as we are seeing the innocent people being massacred in Wau, that's more than too much a failure that can't fit in any denial bag.

With the SPLM/A-IO as a bystander, being at a constant political humiliation from the arrival day of its Chairman and C-in-C Dr. Riek Machar nor there is anything has changed by the formation of TGoNU which is something Mr. Kiir and the JCE want to proof and emphasize that the TGoNU and the IGAD plus are just ink on papers with no effect whatsoever. The road ahead is still gloomy, uncertain and it is likely that the SPLM/A-IO will continue with that approach of non-confrontation, turning its cheeks to be slapped 77 times until Mr. Kiir and his JCE got a little sober and rational which they will do, not for the love of fear of the SPLM/A-IO but definitely because of the crumbling economic situation, people going hungry, broke and the country is ultimately bankrupted. Well it is never an option choosing one's ego and arrogance over a country imminent collapse if they can help it anyway.

June 30, 2016
In a Nutshell

After the bloody Wau massacre should we deny that there is a national outcry in this country against the systematic injustice of the Kiir-JCE expansionist establishment and that this outcry is just lacking the right leader that can consolidate it and give it an inclusive meaning, a national face and lead it to victory? Is Dr. Machar losing it and falling into the same gentleman's agreements scenario with the said establishment just like David Yau who once was claiming he was leading a revolution to liberate his people, the Murle from the marginalization and domination of the Kiir-JCE establishment, however, a few months later, the Murle people were escorted back to the same bitter status quo while Yau has made his way to be a member of the corrupt rich political establishment?

Is an emergence of a new revolutionist leader possible, a leader who will be able and capable to consolidate this uncoordinated voices against injustices from Malakal and Nasir in upper Nile to Yambio and Mundri in Equatoria to Wau and Tonj in Bar Al-Ghazal to Twi and Akobo in Jonglei? A leader who knows the clear difference between real revolution and the opportunism to power where the later tends to settle for less that accommodates its leaders to any share in power, leaving the establishment of injustice intact and unchanged while the former may not accept any deal or compromise less than the total change of the injustice establishment?

Do the scenario of gentleman's agreements with Kiir-JCE establishment really addresses the roots of the conflict in South Sudan or are they just temporary accommodations and silencing of the voices against the injustice establishment and which at no time will make a U-turn to the same cycle of marginalization, domination and injustice policies? Aren't we looking for a real change in the governing system that can establish a great country of South Sudan based on equal rights? If so, then entertaining the current mindset and tribal approach of Kiir-JCE establishment is a crime we are committing against our own and the future generations of this country.

So we think, we hope and we expect that the Kiir-JCE

establishment will change, regain its South Sudanese heart, bring back its dead conscience to life again and they will come and apology to their own victimized brethren and say; sorry we are lost and deeply drawn by power, greed and selfishness which played with our minds and made us forgot why we all fought for this country and what should this nascent country look like or should be? Well, that is not likely folks, the Kiir-JCE expansionist establishment will continue their tight grip on power, using all the injustice tools and approaches and of course the jobs and titles opportunists from the 64 tribes to reach their absolute tribal rule, same just like what Khartoum was doing to the collective South, Nuba and Darfur which happen to be collectively the unaware majority in the former united Sudan until later when the ruling minority in Khartoum deeply installed themselves and became impossible to be removed or shaken, too late.

As we all work to avoid war and violence between the sections of one nation but alas, when the Kiir-JCE establishment is determined to impose their discrimination and expansionist approach, grabbing people lands and swallowing people rights then the strategy of turning one's two cheeks 7 times for each to be slapped 77 times or the non-confrontation approach is never an option to our people. Neither the JMEC, IGAD and Troika has any effective enforcement mechanism to this so-called IGAD Plus and in the long run, we may find ourselves automatically back to the bloody square one, that is a high probability.

Well, the real issue here is that we are not dealing with a stranger as an enemy but our enemy is one of us, they know our fears, they know our thoughts and they know what we want and accordingly they are dealing with us with knowledge, denying the facts and truth at will and choosing chaos and hostility as a method to terrorize the rest of us to achieve their selfish gains. They are testing their mechanical majority whether they can crush everyone, be might and own the whole country, things that will never succeed rather than putting innocent lives in constant danger and the country into uncertain future.

July 6, 2016
In a Nutshell

South Sudan road back to normalcy and health is not furnished with love roses and sweet candies as some of us may think, it is a gradual process with no guarantees at all that it will happen smoothly all the way without bloody interruptions or at worst, a total disruption of the whole process. Those who recall the nature and circumstances leading to the whole peace agreement may knew that this peace has many enemies and opponents, both internally and externally as well and hence any disruption or provocations are not necessarily SPLM/A-IO or IG originated, we have many political actors in Juba with many conflicted interests that if given a chance they won't hesitate to blow off the whole process.

The culture of political assassinations is a strange and dangerous trend in South Sudan and in a country awash with guns and lawlessness, no one is barely safe, not even those who seem to be enjoying it now. However, the fact that we must accept with resilience is that, when soldiers go to war in defense of their nations and countries, death casualties are almost a certainty even in the ranks of the most brave, well trained and armor-supported armies of the advanced world and hence the SPLM/A-IO supporters must know that they just have entered an enemy zone and that it won't be all sweet and smiles and that some prying eyes and hate-filled hearts are somewhere in the lawless city waiting to take down the most vulnerable and if possible, the most valuable target that would make the whole peace process crumble at no time.

Well, some blame must be directed to the SPLM/A-IO leadership as it seems that they have entered the city with the same South Sudanese weakness and less precaution habit, roaming the city without an adequate security and safety plan of their own, eating and drinking from the hotels and restaurants of the enemy of yesterday without the slightest doubt of what is beneath the hearts of the fake smiling faces. Well, I know that we tend to ignore many things but I must admit that the South Sudan of today is not the South Sudan of yesterday and many things have dramatically changed and hence, safety is a personal responsibility first before it is a Riek Machar's weakness or SPLM/A-IO's responsibility.

However, there is a need for an effective security plan and immediate enforcement throughout Juba if not the whole country, a joint plan by the TGoNU partners backed by the regional and international partners and as a matter of fact Juba is not impossible to be secured neither the unknown gunmen are truly unknown. They are within Juba, somewhere and their actions are not that of lone wolf actors as they seem to be very well organized and with specified and well-selected targets, mostly politically motivated killings. Juba has many mafias-like underground networks, some may be linked to the ruling establishment security apparatus and acting on their orders, some are for all sorts of money crimes and laundering, some are hit men from the regional neighbors doing business to their clients and hence Juba is never safe for political activists who are vocal in opposing policies of government or the powerful ruling elite and this isn't a new trend in East Africa.

Well, even though he is tightly secured by his clan as presidential guards in his vast J1 palace, president Kiir should be worried about the security of Juba if not the whole country even in terms of attracting regional and international financial investments and hence he shouldn't let his security boys spoil the investment and business atmosphere of Juba and turning it into fear and crime city. No investors whatsoever will ever choose as an investment destination, a city where unknown gunmen freely kidnap, rob and kill businessmen and political activists at a daylight and it seems that out of ignorance, the ruling establishment in this country is hanging its own neck with ropes of their own making.

As for Dr. Machar and the SPLM/A-IO leadership down the line of the ranks and files, the recent killing of their own officers has a clear message that they should take seriously and it is about time and how cautious is everyone that should at least prevent who is next. SPLM/A-IO has difficult yet a worthy mission to accomplish and people shouldn't backtrack from the peace process because of some anti-peace elements terrorizing SPLM/A-IO members. Even if the SPLM/A-IO has opted to return to war, the death won't stop but in fact it would just increase and the people who are calling us to go back to war may just refresh their minds a bit and recall the whole situation of no winner in the three years' civil war that we are trying to end now. While taking all the necessary security and safety measures, we must never let the enemies of peace and South Sudan to win, let us finish what we have started, at least with less cost.

July 9, 2016
In a Nutshell

Whatever happens yesterday indicates a clear risk to the entire leadership of the SPLM/A-IO and their limited protection unit and such conspiracies can't be fitted in the narrative of mere confrontations between soldiers of the two rival factions without a backing plan from the higher authority of the SPLM/A-IG. If he wanted to, Paul Malong could have stopped the fire immediately after its breakout between his soldiers and those of the SPLM/A-IO and a similar move could be followed by Gen. Gatwech Dual if the matter was truly a quarrel or disagreement between the soldiers. Ironically enough, the fight was let on to continue for hours and most types of the heavy weapons were used resulting in high unnecessary causalities on both sides and many young precious lives were claimed. The questions of course are; Why the fight wasn't contained until the time it became clear to the perpetrators that their plan haven't worked as projected and that the situation is escalating to another worse bloody scenario that they may lose control of and accordingly they have to let Dr. Machar to go back to his compound and with this move Juba was saved if not the entire South Sudan from exploding into a new bloodshed worse than before.

Whether the objective of yesterday well-calculated plot was to assassinate or arrest Dr. Machar, the truth is that this isn't a new plan or a mere coincidence but a one that has been planned in advance before Dr. Machar arrival to Juba. How could one accept the very idea that the president soldiers wouldn't respect the sanctity of J1? How could the SPLA-IO soldiers start a fire on the news of the alleged arrest of Dr. Machar before verifying the reliability and truthfulness of the news from their top commanders and the SPLM/A-IO leadership whom several members were at the presidential palace at the same time? A phone call to Ambassador Ezekiel Lul or Dr. Machar himself could have cleared the confusion and verified the news of the alleged arrest and hence the narrative that the fire was started by the SPLM/A-IO soldiers amid the news of the arrest of their Chairman doesn't hold waters and Gen. Paul Malong, Kuol Manyang and of course Ateny Wek Ateny and Mading Ngor Akech may need to come with a better version of covering lie.

The lives of South Sudanese are being put into constant danger by people who still refuse the fact that Dr. Machar's life and security is a matter of grave national security concern in this country and that any attempt for a foul play will be a complete explosion that won't be confined only in J1 or Juba but it will be a bloody explosion everywhere in this country and wherever there is South Sudanese. Therefore, I argue our shallow minded tribalist who's their tribal thinking is failing to comprehend the immediate dire consequences and implications on any conspiracies in regard to security and life of Dr. Machar to revisit how the Rwanda genocide started and the fact that the fire they about to set aflame would not be like the 2013 nor it will take us only three years, it could mean the real doom to South Sudan. Please let South Sudanese live in peace and forget about your hungry tribal ego.

Sometimes one does wonder whether our highly educated leader of SPLM/A-IO Dr. Machar is the right fit to fight with the criminal mentality of Kiir-Awan communist regime and this is for the obvious reason that Mr. Machar is no match in terms of making up conspiracy theories nor in waging bloody destructive warfare that doesn't spare a soul whatsoever and this has been an asset and opportunity to his arch enemies while it has been a grave risk and loss to himself and his supporters throughout the 35 years he has been leading his many wars against the bias and the odds in criminal-minded SPLM/A tribal leadership.

Mr. Machar is a good man who was placed by the circumstances of South Sudan liberation struggle in a sensitive position with people who in fact didn't mean the fight for South Sudanese liberation and throughout his fights with the bias within the SPLM/A leadership, the man has refused to shape a constant idea about the people whom he has been fighting with within the top echelon of the SPLM/A and as well failed in defining the mentality of his rival peers as a very dangerous one neither he has gathered the right tools and techniques to fight it till change or finish. He has been in and out, reconciling and forgiving with the same mafia who already had defined a path and a destination to him and whoever is supporting his many movements until this hour.

With South Sudan at a crossroads and the war taking a different turn, I do believe it is the time Mr. Machar should step aside or change his good heart to be able to fight the criminal mentality at the top echelon of power otherwise he will always experience only defeat and at the end of the day it may cost him so dearly. I do believe it is time for the change. The yesterday bloody fight of his soldiers and Awan-Kiir's indicate the grave danger that is around him and his few forces in Juba and should things turn for worse without an effective change in the current strategy and the capacity of his forces, the outcomes clearly won't be on his favor. I argue the Chairman of the SPLM/A-IO Dr. Machar to change his strategies regarding his safety and the safety of his supporters and most importantly he must define accurately the dangerous mentality he is dealing with otherwise the danger would spare no one.

July 10, 2016
In a Nutshell

The likely scenarios:

I- I don't believe up to this point that the situation is no longer intentional and if there will be a will from the two warring parties to bring the fighting to a halt. If this escalation is from Paul Malong and Koul Manyang without the approval of Kiir then expect a rift between the three otherwise the bucks of lies stop here.

2- The SPLA-IG do believe that they are well prepared, well-armed and out numbering the SPLA-IO and hence they believe they will bring a quick defeat to the SPLA-IO and capture their leadership. This is not going to happen; the IO forces are going to resist until the last man or until a re-enforcement arrive.

3- Re-enforcements to both rival parties may be already moving towards Juba. and the likelihood of the eruption of military confrontations in different parts of the country

4-The International Community may move in to de-escalate the situation but still I don't know how.

5-The SPLA-IO may not be alone in this fight; they could be joined by many opposing forces to Kiir regime which means the government forces may disintegrate.

6-UN should be watching the possibility of civilians being targeted and should open and secure routes for them to escape to heavy protected safety sites.

7- I don't know whether Paul Malong and Kuol Manyang will be still fighting for the sake of keeping Kiir in power, maybe for the time being.

8-Those who have been talking about "Salva Kiir must go" have a golden chance by now.

9-As long as the fighting continues, civilians who think may be targeted because of their ethnicity should leave their homes and hotels to UN protection.

10- We should not doubt that we are back to full scale war worse than the 2013.

July 11, 2016
In a Nutshell

We all have to take note today from the way the SPLM/A-IO base was attacked Sunday, July 10th, 2016. We all thought that Juba demilitarization plan was a fact and that the cease-fire monitoring team was effective or the cease-fire itself is holding and binding and not forgetting those non-major confrontations as real threats to the agreement and that the JMEC wouldn't hide it useless tail when Kiir exposes how he has been lying ever since. Today our doubts and concerns were proven right, doubts about whether Juba is truly demilitarized and whether the agreed number of forces allowed for both parties are exact and that there is a plan B for Malong and Kuol that's totally opposite to the demilitarization plan.

In their second attempt to inflict harm to the leadership of SPLM/A-IO and its 1300 strong protection unit, the heaviness of the attack and the timing were meant to totally wipe out the whole entire SPLM/A-IO base and leave them between dead, wounded and captured and as we have seen some of them dancing here in the Facebook about the imminent destruction of SPLM/A-IO boys and sure captured of their leadership. Such a day dreaming and illusion was quickly interrupted by the SPLM/A-IO brave young men and proven to be failed mission in which in few hours, the whole city was deserted to UN protection camps, fights from and to Juba were canceled and Juba was a ghost city for the whole day where the heavy attack on SPLM/A-IO positions was going on, supported by Hilocaptors gunships, battle tanks, heavy artillery but all went in vain. By the end of the day, Malong army suffered defections as never before and those who didn't have a chance to join the SPLM/A-IO before, did seize this rare moment and as a result, the SPLM/A-IO gained more military might and power than it was two days ago

This Monday morning, we thought Malong and Kuol Manyang will come and continue with their unwarranted provocations that are aimed in failing the peace process. However, until this hours Juba is reported to be calm and insecurely quiet and whether they will start it again sooner or later, Kuol and Malong may have realized their miscalculations and that the war they are about to pursue is very counter-productive to their rule and power and that the whole country is truly fed up with their tribal policies, failed leadership and mismanagement in which South Sudan has crumbled and bankrupted.

It is worth mentioning that, from 2005 -2016, death and insecurity have been the talk of the day throughout the country, the economy has collapsed, the social fabric of this nation has been destroyed and our people are divided than before. In the course of full 11 years, the Kiir administration has failed in every direction, given the huge financial resources from the oil sector and the vast funding opportunities from the international financial institutions who were ready to help build the nascent nation. He miserably failed to utilize such vast resources and great opportunities and I wonder whether he will ever get such a chance in whatever time left from his rule. My concluded opinion about Kiir is that even if you made him drink gold he will never produce gold and history will mark my words. At the same note, Uganda of Museveni may also realize that Kiir is the problem and accordingly it has declared that it has no intention to intervene and help a proven failed government and whether this is true or not, the fact is that Juba is bankrupted and has no blood dollars to hire more "Hire-to-Kill" armies or mercenaries.

Another possible reason is that, while the SPLM/A-IO military re-enforcement maybe on the way to Juba or eruption of other military confrontations around the country, a likelihood of full-scale war is truly on sight, one that's far more destructive than that of 2013. First, because the pretext that the 2013 war was fought upon as Nuer Vs. Dinka is no more the case. This coming war is more inclusive and brings about the whole country against a proven failed leadership, divisive ruling clique, financial and morally corrupt leadership to an extent that has placed the country in a very ugly image only God knows its true face.

The South Sudanese people are fed up, from Wau and Tonj in greater Bar Al-Gazal, Malakal and Bentiu in greater Upper Nile, to Mundri and Yambio in greater Equatoria and Kiir rule has generated troubles and opposing forces everywhere in this country that are enough to constitute a national front against his failed rule, that is if we add the fact that the country has totally failed in terms of socio-economic and political dimensions. South Sudan today is absolutely Zero and if I was Kiir I could just resign and save the little water in may face if he truly got any drop left. These various reasons and others, make a return to war for Kiir a complete suicide mission. Well, rescuing Kiir also is a double-edged sword, while it is necessary for the country, it is a certain liability, Kiir is no more trustworthy and empowering him is like tying a rope in one own neck, sadly.

How does it really cost to rewind the whole bloody tape to its beginning just tp prove a useless tribal ego that will never win in this country? Who will ever trust the Junta in their fake dealings? However, SPLM/A-IO given the powerful position it demonstrated today, it has no fear if it continued with the same strong position, insisting on the implementation of the peace process from the position of righteous and powerful. Our people must accept that the sacrifices of our people are never going to end in vain and that this path to victory is never backtracked and hence, the confused Kiir camp can also be dealt with from power and truth position, point blank. It is never up to Kiir and his confused camp, we are all in it.

Status Post
July 14, 2016

Chuar Juet Jock
April 23, 2016

Does the SPLM/A-IO have any safety exit strategy from Juba and a re-enforcement plan in case things won't work out given the continuous delay tactics to the arrival of its leader? The International community, JMEC, IGAD can't do a thing if a military confrontations are to be the case at any time and space. Don't just put you neck in the trap without a plan B.

#Chuarezkoff,
April 23rd, 2016

July 16, 2016
In a Nutshell

Everlasting peace is the one emerges from a position of strength not the one that depends on the mercy of your rival. This is something Dr. Machar has missed and neglected from the very inception of 2013 crisis. Luckily, has was pushed out from power with the thousands of

Nuer who were outraged by the mass killings of their loved ones, a mistake from Salva Kiir that Machar failed to invest effectively and accurately. No one can deny that the balance of power in the early days of the armed confrontations between SPLM/A-IO and SPLM-IG was clearly shifted on the side of SPLM/A-IO evidenced in the swift capture of both Bor, Malakal and Bentiu and many other cities even though the movement was gravely lacking heavy weapons by the time. However, the SPLM/A-IO failed miserably in keeping this momentum by not turning it into a constant powerful military movement aimed at a total dislodging Kiir from power and as result, the huge manpower that turned out to fight Kiir, motivated and charged by the 2013 massacres was escorted back to ineffectiveness and confusion.

Dr. Machar still refuse to have a final conviction that the solution to his historical problem with Kuol Manyang and Makuei Lueth in regard to 1991 won't be attained through a soft approach and scientific solutions alone and that the ruling establishment in J1 don't understand any other peaceful approach to salvage the political differences or the issues of power and resources sharing in the country but the language of the gun and killings as the only approach to bring everyone on a bending knee to their divisive political project and accordingly while the attention was diverted to a fake political solution through negotiations in Addis Ababa, a paralleled military, police-security state solution was also being secretly put into effect.

Through the negotiations period in Addis Ababa, both Kuol Manayang and Paul Malong were actively busy building a huge military arsenal and training a huge armies that should have no match within the country if not within the region and while they were spending 100s of $ millions if not $billions in this secret arms and weapons and a booming business of weapons dealings through our bad guys in East Africa and their dealers in the world, the country was intentionally left socio-economically and politically unattended for and this may be as a result of the desire to address the local threats to the divisive political project and which the Nuer were projected as the first threat before embarking on building South Sudan on this certain political approach and governance system.

If apologies and forgiveness has an effect in solving the historical grudges between Dr. Machar and Kuol-Makuei and the rest of his faceless enemies then Dr. Machar first apology could have done that, alas all Dr. Machar attempts for a reconciliation were rejected and a goal to eliminate or destroy Machar was set as the final resort whatsoever even at the expenses of losing the whole country and nation. Adding salt to the wounds, Mr. Machar ambition to the presidency has become a new driver that has united the camps of Kuol Manyang-Makuei with the camp of Salva-Malong which means a new alliance of historical grudges and the power struggle are now going hand in hand as the new political formula to advance the ruling establishment agenda.

What Dr. Machar still don't get is that there is no place for him in Juba through a soft approach that is really not well backed up by a real military power and effective strategy and that neither the paper promises and guarantees from the international community has advantage for him as we have seen and that his life will always be a target of his arch enemies at any time and space. To have a real place on the table of the political power in South Sudan, he must build his army and rely on it at any political compromise, the same way Malong Awan and Kuol Manyang are doing. A new military approach indicates that Kuol with David Yau and possibly Lul Ruai Koang and Gordon Buay are building a military alliance that is aimed to answer the question of the threat posed by the Lou Nuer, a fundamental front to Mr. Machar given Ugandan withdrawal. Well, this is just a bit of the possible inclusive military strategy to win militarily and to enhance the divisive political project and power consolidation. What does the SPLM/A-IO know about this, do they have a counter plan and military strategy? Or is it the cry for unsustainable peace as always?

Diplomatically, Mr. Machar should not accept being cornered in the regional sphere, he need to move actively and build strong political and military ties with some powerful regional powers as Mr. Kiir is doing through Museveni and other in the East Africa region. Days before Juba clashes, Mr. Kiir was in both Kigali and Kampala and only God knows what was his plans while his unknown gunmen were initiating the conspiracy that was yet to be completed in his presence at J1. Such a grave conspiracy to eliminate Dr. Riek can't be initiated and executed without some regional and international mobilization and lobbying as we have seen from the timing of Dr. Reeves and the Kiir meetings with Museveni plus other diplomatic activities to both Ethiopia and Sudan.

Undoubtedly, much is needed in terms of planning and strategizing for the SPML/A-IO to be a peace maker in South Sudan. It must never beg for peace or depend on the mercy of SPLM/A-IG whatever may happen because this simply would never be a better approach to safeguards any peace deal rather than it is storing a war to be fought in another time. The problem in South Sudan is not any longer a local issue, and the Dinka and Nuer will be kept killing each other for a while through local, regional and international fanning and economic interests and the gap and rivalry between the two main powerful tribes is widening and will be kept in such a direction until the last link is no more. Well, blamed it to the defiant and arrogant

J1 and JCE ruling establishment and their divisive political project and not necessarily on Mr. Machar.

Locally, Mr. Machar must seize the political opportunities provided to him by Mr. Kiir failed national approach and use them to build an inclusive better national approach. Politics is an active endeavor and you must keep your mind at the continuous scan, identifying possible threats, seizing new opportunities and making moves to make sure you are achieving your political objective. You can't wake up suddenly at your rival bullets or victories and still claim that you want to survive in the political scene.

July 19, 2016
In a Nutshell

Sorry my South Sudanese people and as much as we wished for peace to prevail and our broken lives to get a chance to be rebuild and our bleeding wounds to get time for healing only that our Gelweang-led country is slowly and surely being taken to a complete destruction and disintegration, Sadly.

It is unfortunate that we have ended this way but of course not all of us are in regrets to what is happening in South Sudan and as we have seen some are celebrating and calling it victory, some are seeing it a source of pride and most are on it as a business and opportunism of all sorts. I believe up to this point, any attempt to mend our house as South Sudanese is becoming extremely difficult and a lot of doubts are being casted on our collective future. While we insist on the fundamental call that no one whatsoever that should destroy a whole nation and country just because of his/her hate to a certain individual or ethnicity be it for personal or political reason, we feel the hate against Dr. Machar from certain individuals or group(s) is the main reasons behind the total destruction of South

Sudan. This largely and widely evidenced and truly is illogical and doesn't make sense and hence the fact of the matter is that Mr. Machar is just a mere scapegoat to a very divisive project aimed on complete stealing of this country from those who collectively fought for its liberation, the people of South Sudan.

I call it stealing and grand theft because if it wasn't so, the people who were intended to be liberated and freed can't be the same people that are dying and suffering on daily basis since day one of the hard won independence. There is no liberation movement in this world ever done that, turning its weapons against the very people it claimed to liberate only the SPLM/A.

A bit of statistics on the scale of massive mortality rate, whether from the direct causes of the war or its related effects, persistence insecurity, diseases, hunger show that through the sad 11 years, from 2005-2016 show the death tolls in this nation may have exceeded the one we have paid collectively for the liberation war estimated to be 2.5 million precious souls. Why our people should continue to die at this massive scale in the time of an independent South Sudan?

Sadly, hopes that this continuous death through war, tribal or political conflicts may stop anytime soon are also diminishing and from the recent indicators from Juba recent bloody clashes which claimed hundreds of young lives, it seems we are heading to the worse to an extent that a return to normalcy and the South Sudan of the good days is becoming more doubtful than ever.

Well, what I know for sure is that the defiance will be the norm from all the two rival camps, the supporters of Mr. Machar will never give up and will fight Mr. Salva, Malong, Kuol, and Makuei until the last man standing. This is not because of Machar as individual as some of those propagandists may try to distract the core issues of the conflict but Mr. Machar represent the opposite of the tyranny, the opposite of tribalism and the real deal that will usher South Sudan to a safe shore. This is a historical conflict that will not go away with the retirement or replacement of Machar but rather than addressing its root causes since SPLM/A's liberation days in 80s, 90s and until it became a government of the day.

With all the huge propaganda from the enemy, no one can deny Machar willingness and keenness for peace to return to South Sudan. He risked it all by accepting to come to Juba with those few young men armed with only light automatic weapons putting his life and the lives of the rest of SPLM/A-IO leadership, the advance team and that small protection unit all in jeopardy. Unfortunately, we and the world around us witnessed the brutal bloody slaughter, how it was conspired, how it was executed and all our doubts and speculations about how credible and honest was Juba ruling establishment in their obligations and commitment towards the peace agreement came but true.

Due to this betrayal from Kiir-JCE establishment to all the efforts waged to achieve peace in the country and to all the commitments done for the sake of South Sudan, we are about to start another bloody chapter worse than the first and all the local, regional and international efforts waged to achieve peace were thrown into waste and the country is back from hopes to frustration and mistrust. In the light of the nearly impossible to be undone mistrust, we must not doubt the keenness and the seriousness of the Kiir-JCE establishment in carrying out their divisive political project and Mr. Machar must never underestimate at any given time and space that his life is at grave risk.

While the international community has watched and

documented who is now to be blamed and what can be done to save the little hope that is left to the peace agreement, the Gelweang-led government is insisting to reject all the plans put forth by the international community to save the ailing country and nation. They are determined with their hate against Dr. Machar, they are determined to defy the international community and they are on the daily killing of the nation and the country and in this, the balkanization of South Sudan is a sure thing nor is the international intervention something can be avoided. Definitely, the Gelweangs are taking us all for a bloody ride. God saves South Sudan.

July 26, 2016
In a Nutshell

After he finished his brother in law Reik Machar, Mr. Taban will come to face the reality of himself and his game in few months to come, something he won't believe he have done and neither the allure of being the second powerful man in the country or the seduction of glory shall be any longer there. If Kiir can't implement the IGAD peace agreement with Dr. Reik Machar, why would he implement it with Gen.Taban who has no military or political backing as Mr. Machar? The fact is, whether Mr. Taban will play it as SPLM/A-IO defector or its new leader, it is a trend that's also doomed because what makes the SPLM/A-IO significant in the political theater of South Sudan is the ARCISS agreement, something he is bound not to implement or even talk about per the conspiracy deal and that's why he is here and not Reik Machar. It doesn't make any sense why would it be possible for Mr. Taban to implement the ARCISS while Mr. Machar wouldn't? This indicates in fact that there is no such a thing as ARCISS agreement to be implemented and this also could be one of the terms of conspiracy deal of Kiir-Taban.

All indicators points to the bitter reality that, Gen. Taban has sold the expensive hard-won peace agreement and stabbed his brother in law Reik Machar fatally in the back and not only that, but willfully attempted to destroy the SPLM/A-IO that represent the huge sacrifices of more than 50,000 precious souls who perished as result of Salva regime massacres and as result of the 3 years armed struggle against the regime between 2013-2016 and still counting until this hour. Well, the logical question is, if a man could betray such multitude high commitments and relationships then what is left for such a man that he cannot betray? Accordingly, does he think he can be trusted by Mr. Salva or those who are using him to destroy himself and his own political base? Why he wouldn't do it again, this time against his new bosses? A lesson he should have learned from the certain fate of double spies in the intelligence industry.

Absolutely he wouldn't be trusted and the ring of the mafia who are in fierce power struggle around J1 won't let him go any further than his terms and time of use and he will shortly be dumped either dead or half alive. This isn't SPLM/A-IO work, it is Mr. Salva "Hotel Coup" and if it is truly an IO arranged succession then the deputy SPLM/A-IO, Mr. Ladu Gore should be the one that replaces Dr. Machar but also this wasn't the case. Shouldn't this also raise Mr. Taban's eyes' brows and make him question the long-term objectives of such a conspiracy and appointment?

A lone wolf within Juba establishment, Mr. Taban neither will have the military or political backing necessary for him to have a place on the table and in such a reality, he can't implement the ARCISS and his removal and being thrown into a waste is high likely after they successfully or failed to use him to destroy Reik and the SPLM/-IO. Imperatively, Mr. Taban will not be able to confront either of both the popular political or the military base of the SPLM/A-IO and hence I don't know how he will sell his peace and political agenda which will be nothing new or different than Salva and JCE's own divisive political project. Well, Gen. Taban will just circle himself around Juba or Wurrap, delivering nothing new but the same stuff of Kiir Mayardit.

However, Mr. Reik and SPLM/A-IO are yet to be confirmed destroyed otherwise, Gen. Taban will be in hot troubled waters and this could be the end of his political career. Contrary to what Kiir and Co. are spreading, the SPLM/A-IO is not destroyed because of this orchestrated coup in Juba but as a matter of fact, the regime has made a significant media and psychological gains out of it and particularly with Dr. Machar in hiding, everything seem to the ordinary mind that Mr. Salva has finally won the war, well in real sense, that's not true. Mr. Kiir and the country may just wake up anytime soon to a sure new hell.

While the hunt for Mr. Machar intensify to eliminate him so the whole conspiracy could succeed and sealed, the possibility of Mr. Machar coming back stronger and more determined to wage a full-scale war to oust Mr. Salva is high likely. That's, the war may just take a worse turn, where second chances for trust and benefit of the doubt are not likely. Well, we need peace but I must be honest that I don't see a peace in the current political situation created by the power struggle in Juba. Let us wait how it will turn out.

July 27, 2016
In a Nutshell

Congratulations to Mathaing Annyor for their newly
appointed commander, Gen. Taban Deng Gai who have
defected to Kiir camp without a single soldier
accompanying him from the gallant SPLM/A-IO forces.
As of today, all the military commanders and the vast
popular political base of the SPLM/A-IO are intact behind
the next president of South Sudan. Dr. Machar Dorghon.
This time and around the SPLM/A-IO must leave Kiir out
of the plan because he has chosen to dump the August
2015 uneasy compromise that has left him as head of state
even for the projected 18 months by ARCISS. Well, no
regrets whatsoever and he has just offered SPLM/A-IO a
great service and to himself, a great disservice, therefore
and as for now, the "Kiir Must GO" is initiated again,
strongly and powerful as never before as the slogan and
the objective of this final phase of "Kiir must go".

Undoubtedly, Gen. Taban is here to ruthlessly defend his
new glory and power as FVP, he is expected to do all he
can to keep his new position and hence he is projected to
command, this time and around, the Mathiang Annyor and
the rest of the Gelweang militia in an attempt to crush the
SPLM/A-IO, militarily and politically and if you know
Gen. Taban then you may agree with me that he could
prove to be more ruthless than Paul Malong or Mathews
Puljang and that he will hunt down the SPLM/A-IO
wherever they are until they all submit to him and of
course to Kiir. Well, make no mistake about it that the
culture of political assassinations and the unknown
gunmen my just turn to worse until we see a clear winner
in this war of two faces, a one for power struggle versus
the one for reforms and change in the country.

Well, don't ever think that the already complicated political situation is meant to be reversed back to the post-Taban appointment era; this is not likely to happen even though they have told you if Mr. Machar has made it back to Juba today he will be re-instated back to his position. That's a big lie that even Mr. Machar won't buy if he made it out safe from the ongoing intensive hunt aimed at his elimination, in fact, one of the reasons he is being hunted down is to prevent him from waging a full-scale war that could last until Salva is no more. Contrary to what he may believe, Mr. Salva has offered Mr. Machar another golden chance to finish his objective of " Kiir must go" which is already half way, a job that wouldn't be more difficult than at its inception in 2013, given the current state of affairs.

Nonetheless, if you choose to differ with me in this analysis, then let us speculate a bit on the likely scenarios that may end our current political row; if we projected that our people mode is ready to buy anything for now for the sake of peace and hence yield to Gen. Taban takeover as long as he is providing alternative leadership that may bring the divided country back again to unity and harmony, given Kiir's political camp mode change because of the absence of Dr. Machar in active political scene. Do you think such a scenario is likely? Well, if not then, the alternative scenario is that of Dr. Machar coming back more strongly and serious than before in his objective of "Kiir must go" which means another lengthy war without compromises given the recent broken trust and promises.

Well, this or that, agree with me or not, Kiir has just made things more complicated than before; would he dump Taban if Mr. Machar came back from his hideout or re-instate Machar as a result of a new agreement? Can the SPLM/A-IO reconcile with the coup plotters? Well, all these questions point to the fact, the SPLM/A-IO led by Dr. Reik has not been given any other options left but the sure resistance to the attempt to destroy it and the ARCISS agreement.

July 29, 2016
In a Nutshell

The bizarre of Gen. Taban shouldn't be our focus and it shouldn't divert our minds to a meaningless war with a delusional enemy. Nothing new in Juba, no new army that has defected with a mighty force that we should fear but as we know, only bunch of opportunists who has nothing with them in Juba but their bags. Absolutely nothing of any political or military significant value only the extensive noise they are making out of it. They wish if the SPLM/A-IO could just disappear with a fake magic of "Taban" and they are in false celebrations just like they have been doing when they were shooting dangerously all over Juba skies with heavy artillery upon the fabricated news that they have finally got the heads of Dr. Riek Machar and Gen. Gatwech Dual. Well, I heard yesterday that some of them almost died with heart attack and stomachache when they surely heard the brave voice of people leader Dr. Machar on Aljazeera, well until this hour, some are even still sick in disbelief. Dr. Machar is alive and coming back to kick some miserable liars.

Imperatively, what we need to focus on is who is with the SPLM/A-IO in this hour and who is with the defected opportunists and what are their covert activities to confuse and sabotage the SPLM/A-IO political base or their attempts to set up the SPLM/A-IO military wing. They are on the move recruiting and buying people through jobs and positions and with empty promises of fake peace when the logical question is how can someone who is destroying an internationally supervised and guaranteed peace agreement come the other way around trying to sell you nothing but big lie in the name of fake peace after they shamelessly sold the hard-won peace agreement that was meant to achieve a needed transformation and an inclusive change in the whole country just for a FVP post, a bag of few non-key ministers posts, and some rotten executive positions.

Well, let us all be aware that, the most destructive enemy of the SPLM/A-IO has been always from within, doing the enormous harm and destruction from within since 2013 and if the SPLM/A-IO have to succeed this time and around it must distill its ranks and purify its files from those who have been working as source of confusion and failures. If such a measure has been in place since 2013, failure could be that of SPLM/A-IO neither politically nor militarily but this has been the contrary, we were cheated at and played with by individuals whom we have glorified and given the best of our trust and confidence, not only that we have trusted them with the most sensitive positions and information, unfortunately.

Our opportunists were quick and cunning enough and were holding the movement a hostage without military and political advancement. They were quick to surround Dr. Machar from every corner, feeding him false advice and information while at the same time they were building a strong alliance with Kiir regime behind the scene. This is evidenced in the conspiracy that has resulted in Gen. Peter Gatdet and Gen. Gathoth Gatkuoth being fired from the movement in a time when the SPLM/A-IO need them the most. This and other political and military internal rifts were the work of our opportunists within the SPLM/A-IO aimed at destroying the movement from within.

Now, shouldn't the defected opportunists be ashamed talking about their selfish interests based rhetoric in the name of fake peace when young girls and elderly women of ethnic Nuer are being systematically raped within the vicinity of UN and J1 and when the Nuer people of Leer town being starved to death and are on the run being hunted in the bushes. Make no mistake about it, real peace is on the way, a fair, balanced and inclusive peace that is meant not only for certain individual personal interests but to overhaul the whole decayed system of governance and the ailing institutions of the crumbled country. The international community is being tested again and whether they will continue to bury their heads deep down into the sand like they did throughout the deadly incidents of July 8, 9, 10 and 11th respectively and which the cowards in Juba were enjoying showing their heavy muscles on that small protection force of SPLM/A-IO send there as a gesture of peace. What a shame?

Well, in case you got almost cheated that the SPLM/A-IO and its Chairman Dr. Riek Machar are all but done and over. Well, stay your ground unmoved simply because these are illusions made in Juba and will always stay and die in Juba, a matter of time until the fogs clears in the illusionists' minds. Peace isn't here yet and when these two destructive different faces of the mentality of SPLM/A-IG that justifies whatever wrong they do and think and in the same time, quickly and relentlessly dismisses and unjustified whatever right the SPLM/A-IO think and believe as false and impossible are brought to reasoning and sanity, then make no mistake that this country shall then prospers in peace and harmony and until then, take a note.

This is clearly demonstrated in this instance; despite the huge failure of president Kiir leadership evidenced clearly in our current miserable socio-economic and political affairs, our brothers and sisters in SPLM/A-IG are almost ready to put their lives on the line in rejection of our logical call that Mr. Kiir needs to resign and give a chance for someone else who has the competency and capacity to run and develop the country, a process that is done in all the democratic countries. However, in their attempt to stay in power regardless of their clear failures, they have resorted to a strategy of confusion and propaganda to evade the real causes and reasons behind the current political row since its inception in 2013 and its drastic aftermath war that has crumbled the country and the nation. Well, ironically enough, they are giving themselves the right to replace Mr. Machar and not only that to administer his party, appointing and replacing his own successors, what a mentality? Well most of us think that this stop with Machar alas it is not.

August 2, 2016
In a Nutshell

I know that we South Sudanese are tired of war and only that the people in J1 and Bilpam1 seem to have made the war their daily bread since 2013 and as long as they are there, forget about a permanent peace in this country. Well, while they have hanged it all over Dr. Machar, they surely need to know that Machar is not going anywhere anytime soon, like or not, he will be here as long as God want him to be and if you have associated your exclusive peace with his fate than make no mistake about it, you will wait too long.

The irony of those who scapegoat Dr. Machar for everything in this country is that either their minds are short to point to where or to who make the decisions and policies that brought the war and kept it aflame since 2013. Mr. Machar in last April brought peace to Juba in a golden plate yet for it to be slaughtered at daylight by the enemies of peace who sworn to Nhialic that Reik Machar will never be a president in their lifetime or under their watch.

Accordingly, Mr. Machar has now been forced to have only one option, which is to bring the needed change and reforms by force if he can or die as a brave man while fighting his arch enemies and this time and around I believe Mr. Machar will never underestimate or ignore the full willingness of his enemies if they got another chance or window to eliminate him.

In case you may still have some doubts, Gen. Kiir already declared a war and dismantled the August peace agreement and not only that, he has shown us the way forward based on his divisive political approach written for him by his JCE and with the backing of his regional and international friends. Kiir as well is not giving any room neither to the Holy Bible nor to the political game to bring peace to South Sudan and this is evidenced in his absolute refusal of many calls and mediations of influential local and international religious leaders as well as political figures. Well, I might agree with many of our intellectuals that Kiir doesn't control what is taking place in the country and maybe he is a victim of his immediate powerful inner circle, well, whether this assumption is true or not, those inner circle are finishing him and are not protecting him but waiting to grab the power from him and hence they are against the new order of power brought by the peace agreement.

Rarely in the history of South Sudan since the days of Samuel Gai Tut that a politician has to give up his post, luxurious and lavish lifestyle and join his ordinary people in the struggle for justice. Well, Dr. Lam Akol has done it folks yet again in a time of a real call to duty to save this nation and country from our own greed. Kiir cannot be a man enough by grabbing his own brothers' land when he is letting our land in Abyei being grabbed and taken at his watches and if this is not the peak of cowardice than what it is? A million thumb ups to Dr. Lam Akol.

Well, South Sudan political turmoil is finally taking a shape towards a national struggle for some meaningful change and I can see the ranks and file of our politicians are being shaken and distilled between true cowards and real patriots. The future of South Sudan should be a concern for all of us alas not all of us can see the danger ahead, it is about time.

August 2, 2016
In a Nutshell

Now with the war has been switched smartly to the SPLM/A-IO house so it destroys itself from within, fighting for an empty bone without a bit of meat or kill themselves over the leftover from Kiir-JCE power table amid the blindness of the opportunists, it seems as it is heading there, to the projected or programmed destination by of course, the political colt in charge, the JCE. Well, expect some success to this conspiracy since we are not all men and women of principles nor we have the needed capacity to reason and identifies the long term dire consequences of the Kiir-Taban-JCE conspiracy. I wished Mr. Machar has reached to people who can tell him how things really were then they use to seem but the system in SPLM/A-IO is no better than SPLM/A-IG at least at some extent, I must be honest.

Well, my concern is how our political wolves who were used to stage the JCE-sponsored coup against the hard-won peace agreement and its champion Dr. Reik Machar will be heading to our political and military bases in order to dismantle and destroy them both from within, an objective they can survive or succeed without. Well even though the divide to rule or conquer is an old strategy, old enough just like the history of humankind itself, albeit its effectiveness as a strategy to divide and rule never worn out and particularly when it is being applied in a tribal and clan structured society as of Nuer in particular and South Sudanese in general.

I haven't the slightest doubt that Mr. Taban Deng and Lol Gatkuoth and countless others in disguise are coming to divide the already embattled Nuer community with the approach "it is our time to eat" of that famous story of the Kenyan whistle blower, Michela Wrong and hence if they haven't already dispatched their disguised agents to penetrate the community and divide it through expensive promises, offers of jobs, promotions, positions and financial incentives for their clan and tribesmen first and those jobs seekers in general. Taban and Lol have a long observed political alliance that is mostly built based on common interests of the two, the Jikanyism of both and of course the oil money when Mr. Taban was then a governor of the rich Unity state. With Taban being from Western Jikany Nuer and Lol from Eastern, their approach to divide the Nuer will be likely by pulling the Jikany Nuer in sort of "our time to eat" or rule philosophy, the same approach that was applied by a section of Bull Nuer in their alliance with Kiir throughout the 2013-2015.

However, success of such a divisive approach is also in balance due to the fact that the Jikany Nuer is also a home of a vast support to SPLM/A-IO and its Chairman Dr. Reik Machar and with recent fighting in Nasir being reported, such a divisive policy might not see any light of success except within those trapped in Juba and for reasons that not far than security and safety concerns. Militarily, there is a high likelihood that Gen. Gathoth Gatkuoth and countless others in disguise are part of the conspiracy against SPLM/A-IO and its Chairman Dr. Reik Machar, that is to say that a wide coalition is being pursued to include most of the Nuer politicians within Juba and of course other politicians from other communities who were affiliated with the SPLM/A-IO. Well, I have no doubt that the Taban-Front is consolidating itself in a way or another and through the various means but do wonders not, even the political beggars can form a front.

Well, while such political offensive is being waged to dismantle the SPLM/A-IO political base from within and to force it to shift its allegiance and support from Dr. Reik to Gen. Taban, a paralleled intensive military offensive is being waged against the SPLM/A-IO forces in the Equatoria region and with objective of eliminating its top leadership in the person of Dr. Reik Machar, Gen. Gatwech Dual, Gen. Koang Chuol Raanley, Gen. Martin Kenyi and countless others of top generals, however, it seem the advantage in the battlegrounds is shifting towards the SPLA-IO as the recent news has it that thousands of Equatorians freedom fighters has already joined the ranks of the SPLA-IO and that heavy weapons, tanks, and others military supplies has been captured from the thousands of Mathiang Annyor who been fleeing to UNMISS compound for their lives. It is predicted that the SPLM/A-IO shall thrive in Equatoria region and make it the base for the wind of positive change for all South Sudan. Those who have been dreaming since July 8th of Reik Machar capture or demise, they definitely will dream on for a very long time and learn that to attain power is not by stabbing your movement in the back rather than standing in a solid unity until the glorious objective is achieved.

August 3rd, 2016
In a Nutshell

It been almost a month and the SPLM/A-IO Chairman Dr. Reik Machar is holed up in the bushes of Equatoria luckily resisting and escaping the intensive hunt by the forces of Kiir-JCE. In such a critical situation one would wonders why it took nearly a month without a rescue or reinforcement force being sent by the SPLM/A-IO military headquarters to save its top leadership or I might be behind the news if such a force is under way.

It should be a race with time to save the SPLM/A-IO top leadership as it is with those who are hunting to eliminate them, the faster it is the better. You can't rely on guessing or luck in this sophisticated technological world nor does Kiir-JCE or the Taban-Front want to see Dr. Machar alive so their plans don't get spoiled.

I know there could be logistics and mobility problems in this rainy season, however, nothing amounts to the lives of the top leadership of any organization besides most of the SPLM/A or South Sudanese are used to the rainy season long walk leave alone being a soldier

Kiir intelligence and spies are all over Equatoria region, using all the techniques and technologies to solicit for information leading to whereabouts of Dr. Reik Machar and his colleagues. They are also mobilizing massive military forces that are meant to overwhelm the expected forces of the SPLM/A-IO protecting the top leadership. Well, with that in mind, it is definitely about time and how is the SPLA military is planning to rescue its top leadership otherwise you can't tell what will be next.

With the chairman and the military top generals in the bushes of Equatoria, Pagak can't be that idle and quiet as there no danger to the lives of its leaders. At least they should keep us informed otherwise something is fishy here or unless they have left their fate on the luck and mercy of Kiir-JCE forces, well, that is not an option to resort to at any cost.

September 5 · 2016
In a Nutshell

So how did the UNSC diplomats got the hard stuff into
the brains of the stone-headed government of Kiir Mayar
and made them melt their utter defiance and arrogance in a
matter of days and not only that but softly forced them to
shamelessly swallowed their outburst and tempered
statement "We won't accept even a single soldier". Well,
now they are accepting not only "single soldier" but 4,000
soldiers, Ironic isn't it? I have seen the pictures of Makuei
Lueth laughing so hard and chatting with UNMISS's boss
and one would still wonder where does this man get the
heart and the guts to laugh in such a way in a land where it
is all skulls and skeletons of their own making? Sad indeed!

Whether it is a "Protection or Intervention force" this
hasn't changed the number of the 4000 soldiers stated
from the first day nor it did prevent their sure coming and
so what the hell was all this noise about the so claimed
sovereignty and foreign invasion? Nor does it make sense
that the Kiir regime was all furious about "Intervention
force" but finally consented to the "Protection force" of
the foreign troops to come and protect the South
Sudanese people from their own government "if it is really
still their government and not their killer" and they
wouldn't even ask themselves or the UN diplomats this
simple question: You want to protect who from who?

Well, the answer is here: protecting the South Sudanese
people from their own so-called national government and
from their own so-called national army, since the two are
no longer constitute a national government or national
army respectively and this isn't a baseless claim rather than
it is a true statement backed by a well-documented

systematic power abuse, human rights violations and grave atrocities from either the Kiir's government and his tribal militias. Most of the massacres and grave atrocities committed and still being committed by Kiir regime were and still ethnic-based whether in Greater Upper Nile, Greater Equatoria or against Fertit and Jurchen tribes in Wau and the UNSC is not acting out of the blue but has a solid evidence and well-documented records of grave atrocities that even Kiir himself won't believe it is from his own Mathiang Annyor making.

The need for a national army and the necessity of overhauling all the tribal security organs is paramount to South Sudan peace and stability. This won't be possible but through the ARCISS agreement that the Al-Tabaneen have betrayed and sold out cheaply and with nothing in return but useless and temporary positions of FVP and Petroleum. The current Kuol-Malong tribal militias Mathiang Annyor can't fit to be called or regarded a national army in any form possible leave along their lengthy records of ethnic-based atrocities since the eruption of this war. Al-Tabaneen can't claim that they are implementing the ARCISS or will do so since they are but "Yes Stooges" that won't even say "NO" to anything coming from Kiir & JCE and a month of their own "TGoNU" with Kiir has already shown that as we haven't heard anything about the 28 states or any of the other pressing issues but the usual rhetoric of Riek Machar did this, Riek Machar did that, Pathetic enough!

Well, make no mistake about it, the ARCISS is here to stay and has its defenders, its advocates and those who are ready to die for its implementation in letter and spirit. It is an agreement meant to change this country and its nation for better and hence it can't be sold just for few meaningless positions that won't last longer than Kiir himself. Kiir positions are no permanent, he changes them as he changes his shoes and shirts and accordingly the fate of this country rely on the ARCISS and not on individuals' selfish interests. The SPLM/A-IO under the leadership of Dr. Riek Machar and in alliance with the rest of opposition forces in this country shall either press for the full implementation of the ARCISS or a total regime change. It is not over yet and the regional protection force is not here out of the blue, the UN surely knows that hard times are still ahead for this country and its nation.

August 5, 2016
In a Nutshell

Now Dr. Riek Machar betrayal by few of his very own immediate trustees should teach all of us a lesson and of course shake like no other our old perception that even the Nuer has the same strong loyalty and commitment principles to their leadership leave alone the rest of South Sudanese. Before his arrival to South Sudan capital, Juba in April. The plan to sabotage and derail the peace process and apparently to assassinate him and the rest of the SPLM/A-IO top leadership was already worked out between the government of Kiir and the defectors group of military generals and politicians who vowed to sell it all in order to stop Reik Machar.

The rivalry within the SPLM/A-IO and particularly within the Nuer was what has given Kiir regime the window to derail the peace agreement. Some saw it as a fight for positions rather than an agreement to enact needed reforms to the ailing country and its corruption-ridden and dysfunctional institutions. This wrong perception was strengthened by what is seen as was Dr. Machar attempt to get his job back and all the propaganda smeared around it both from the Kiir regime propaganda machine as well as from the other competing forces within the Nuer political base of SPLM/A-IO.

Well, it was anticipated that the Kiir regime is going to use the disgruntled generals and our never-get-old politicians from the Nuer against Dr. Machar to derail the agreement using their differences and grudges and pit them to fight on who should take what in TGoNU in secret deals and conspiracy theories that has resulted in the drastic event of the bloody July 8th-11th which started with the Murder of SPLM/A-IO officers George and Domach and the subsequent J1 fight and finally the full scale offensive on Sunday July 11th that was meant to slaughter everyone in SPLM/A-IO but mainly the top leadership. Let us speculate a bit on whether the coup against the peace agreement was an insider job that has led to the crack in SPLM/A-IO leadership with Gen Taban Deng as the main suspect or was it a sudden idea generated by the absence of SPLM/A-IO chairman who has been trapped in some hideouts around Juba.

Most if not all of us who have observed the immediate discontent of Gen. Taban Deng Gai being appointed the Minister of Mining and his subsequent resignation as the lead negotiation team of the SPLM/A-IO has predicted something fishy must be in the air and apparently the Gen. saw a betrayal or underestimation from Dr. Machar for his lengthy efforts as the man who mainly negotiated the agreement that installed his brother in law and sister at the second most powerful job in the country. His dissent turned into a plan to get rid of his in law with the help of those who also share with him the same feelings in the person of Amb. Ezekiel Gatkuoth who also may have the same reasoning that he has done a lot in support to his former boss Dr. Machar more than some people within the SPLM/A-IO who were given national minister positions while he was left out. A second group was the group of Gen. Gathoth Gatkuoth, Gabriel Yual Dok, Mario Thour who defected earlier from the SPLM/A-IO and who in turn, signed some secret agreement with Kiir regime through his security advisor Tut Gatluak and only God know what was in those secret agreements as their suspicious arrival to Juba weeks before Reik Machar arrival and the Church incident of the fight between Machar and Gathoth guards.

As we can see a remarkable buildup of multiple enemies to Reik Machar in Juba and all offering a job of getting rid of him to Kiir and who in return toke the advantage and through his vast executive power made the coup possible. Well, the coup against the peace and against TGoNU is a reality now and with all the players aforementioned being part of the Taban-TGoNU reshuffle and the rest shall emerge sooner or later only that it is all confined in Juba and around Mr. Kiir's pillow, it has no effect whatsoever around the country not even in UNMISS' IDPs. In few months from now, things should look differently and we shall come to the full realization that Riek Machar was in fact, the problem or whether he was just a mere scapegoat throughout these, time will not lie.

While Reik Machar and his SPLM/A-IO still retain the political and military base around the country that apparently has grown and risen like never before and if the government believe in crushing them military than this will take another year or two before a clear winner can be declared and by that time I don't know whether the Taban-TGoNU will be still intact, well they have to be very careful for any miscalculation as they have nobody in Juba but only JCE-Kiir's notorious NSS and brutal Mathiang Annyor as their protector and their butcher at the same time. All in all, most indicators show that the country has more political and injustice grievances than the one Mr. Kiir and Co. has in mind. How the 28 states and the status of Malakal will be settled are few among many and new opposition players are adding to the old ones. Dr. Lam Akol and Gen Bakasoro for one and some others influential figures behind the scene. These new Kiir's opponents may form a new alliance with Machar, stronger and diverse front than before, a one that might hit the right national political formula that this country truly needs. Nevertheless, Mr. Kiir, Kuol and Malong for sure will still have some final kicks of the dying horses for some time but the men's rule in the actual sense has but ended.

August 12, 2016
In a Nutshell

Now that the Kiir & Co. are almost cornered by the international community, it seem that their last resort to shield with is the South Sudan's sovereignty, claiming that the regional intervention or protection force that is meant to protect their own people they are systematically murdering, uprooting, raping and subjecting them to forced hunger and all the psychological and mental suffering for a full bloody three years without a bit of shame or even a simple sympathy, is an international invasion and undermining of their claimed country's sovereignty. Shouldn't they ask themselves who in the actual sense sold and undermined the sovereignty of South Sudan? Isn't the same regime reaping what it has been sowing?

Sovereignty has always been used as a shield that protects the rogue regimes in Africa and that stand in the way of the needed urgent help and intervention from the concerned international and regional agencies of human rights, peace and security such as the United Nations Security Council (UNSC) which oversees world peace and security. Ironically enough, it is the same rogue regimes that go load singing about sovereignty and international invasion that have triggered the international involvement in their countries' domestic affairs since they are the ones waging systematic killing of their own people, enforcing policies of grave humans' rights abuses and violations, establishing governance that is based on domination, marginalization and grave injustices to some portions of their own people. When the government become the victimizer and not the protector of the citizen and when states' national powers and resources has been diverted to be used in the privilege of the few, crowning some tribes, religious or political opinions to the status of the dominant while crashing the rest deemed minorities or majorities to nothing but tools of labor, socio-economic and political marginalization and exploitation, there is no other hope but the UNSC intervention, it is an emergency need that should override the claimed sovereignty. Tragically, since Rwanda genocide in 1992, the worst trend of tribal politics in the African states is the desire to completely erase or wipe out the physical presence of the opposite or rival tribe or at least inflict the gravest harm possible using the national powers, capabilities and resources of the state and through bloody massacres, massive uprooting, and wide-scale sexual violence, gangs rape to the women and girls of the opposite tribes and evidently enough, all these grave atrocities has been well documented in the ongoing South Sudan conflict.

What sovereignty Mr. Makuei Lueth is talking about without the slightest shame in his face when they sought willingly and consistently the international intervention by dishonoring the peace agreement brokered by the same international and regional communities? What sovereignty Mr. Makuei Lueth is talking about, when 85% of the nation is being fed by the same UN, International community and NGOs for the last three years? What sovereignty Mr. Makuei Lueth is talking about when South Sudanese women and girls are being systemically gang-raped by the so-called wrongly national army, the SPLA, the notorious security organs and the tribal militias of the regime, Mathiang Annyor? Isn't this the peak of irony and controversy, the peak of political crime and impunity?

Sadly, South Sudan is no exception since the dilemma of most African states is that the they are being ruled and controlled by few manipulative corrupt ruling clique who manipulates the tribally-structured nations, pitting this tribe against that, destroying the very social fabric and cohesion in which any nation stability and peaceful co-existence depends on and in an illiteracy hit society of 73% and where the masses can hardly pick up the meat from the bones it is a certainty that the manipulative few ruling clique always succeed in engaging the various social and political forces in a continuous clash and enmity that they have nothing to gain but only the sure destruction of their social peace and harmony while the only winner here is the same few corrupt ruling clique, running away with people powers and resources, exploiting them as they wish and in collaboration with their business allies everywhere in the corrupt world.

So things went wrong from above, from the top echelon of power where things were meant to be controlled, executed and done right. A national government for all the people of the country, a sun that shines for all and that doesn't listen to the calls or voices of tribalism, sectarianism and all sorts of social and political fragmentation. It is the absence of right and competent national leadership and this by far doesn't mean African nations don't produce brains that have the needed ingredients of good governance and competent leadership, not at all, this is isn't the case. Look at the social media or political debate forums and you will be astonished how debaters on those forums or social media give alternatives bright ideas in good leadership and governance contrary to what is taking place in their respective societies or countries.

The dilemma of African leadership is that we don't have an adequate system of selecting competent leaders nor we have educated political masses that are conscious politically of their political choices that would make a difference in their immediate lives or at countrywide and nationwide levels. African political power is attained either tribally or most often through military coups and where a democratic political process of selecting and vetting the right and competent leaders is rarely the case throughout the continent. if the general assumption is that politicians are wolves in sheep cloth, then we definitely need a process that will tell us who is a real sheep and who is a fake one, a process that should exposes who is who's socio-economic and political programs, vision, policies, character, values...etc. in America and some other democratic countries it take quite a while of an expensive election campaign to a win potential vote of voter, any voter, It is a rigorous process that leaves a stone unturned whether in terms of candidate personal characteristics or socio-economic and political realm unlike our jungle politics where a crucial phenomenon as leadership is completely neglected and underestimated alas we are not heading anywhere without a good head.

Nevertheless, an answer to the African state political dilemma requires both honest, responsible national government and opposition that abstain itself from using and manipulating tribes for cheap political gains and power, that engage the various social and political masses in socio-economic and political programs and are based on nationalism, collective and common citizenry, nation-state building aspirations and not on political divisive project such as the one the JCE political colt is destroying the country and nation of South Sudan with.

August 15, 2016
In a Nutshell

The undeniable fact is that Mr. Kiir & Co. and with unprecedented persistence and hostile reception, pushed Dr. Riek Machar to be the complete rebel they may never have imagined and instead of Dr. Machar and the SPLM/A-IO seeking to share power with Kiir as FVP and partner in power respectively, it is likely now that Mr. Machar will seek the top chair, occupied by Kiir for eleven years without any benefit to the country whatsoever but the complete destruction we have witnessed and the whole world has strongly documented. In his utter madness in the last bloody July, Kiir has given Machar a golden chance and the best opportunity to take over power together with his nationalist comrades from every corner of South Sudan and to establish the democratic, stable and prosperous South Sudan state that we all dreams about.

Another great advantage Kiir has offered to Dr. Machar and the SPLM/A-IO is that; he unconsciously and ignorantly brought the war close to Juba, his seat of power and even closer to his pillow in J1, where his nightmarish has increased double unlike when the bloody war was being fought in all the destroyed cities of Upper Nile region and which was made the scene of war and its people the target of systematic killings and suffering. The disgruntled and grieving Equatorians, whose lands were being grabbed in daylight and their innocent peace loving people being killed with unprecedented impunity are now the backbone of the SPLM/A-IO operations in Equatoria region, fighting for their right to rule this country as presidents and not to age as second vice presidents with zero chance of taking over, a role that has been defined for them here and there and throughout the last 11 years, they have been watching the two regions, Upper Nile and Bar

El-Gazal getting away with the share of lion in everything and in a rare resilience and resolve. However, their resilience and peace loving nature were also taken for granted, mistaken for cowardice and their rights and roles were evaded with persistence impunity. This must stop and must be brought to an end through a federal system of governance championed by SPLM/A-IO the Icons of federalism and democracy, Dr. Riek Machar and Gen. Martin Kenyi.

Kiir and Co. have also awakened the sleeping lions in Equatoria as the Kiir's boys' military operations in Equatoria bushes meant to hunt for Dr. Machar and his small forces turned to be an ignition of a complete revolution that is advancing towards the center of the evil and with the support from all directions of South Sudan, the days of regime in Juba seem to be numbered and this time and around, it is going to be Kiir turn to look for a safety exit strategy and re-enforcement forces. Adding the fuel to the fire, Kiir's militias are proving to be tribalists to the core, burning villages, killing spree and doing the miserable to the people of Equatoria and with nearly 200,000 innocent civilians has fled to neighboring Uganda in the last four weeks alone, a grave indicator that the once peaceful and neutral region in the three years civil war has finally joined the revolution in a full gear, an addition that will have its dire and immediate consequences and may bring an abrupt end to the Kiir & Co. regime as the SPLM.A-IO grows militarily and politically all around the country and this is evident in how the SPLM/A-IO small force have grown in the Equatoria region to be a vast and strong front that's threatening to capture Juba at any time of their own chosen.

As logic and circumstances should dictate, Kiir and Co. should not choose to sink deeper into more madness and defiance at this juncture as it became a norm and business as usual to them to defy anything that is meant to restore peace and stability to the country, twisting and misinterpretation actions and policies of both international community and the SPLM/A-IO aimed to that direction. This time and around they will need to choose wisely between being removed by the forces of the ongoing national revolution for change and reforms spearheaded by the SPLM/A-IO or choose to cooperate fully with International community by allowing the intervention/protection force that is here to protect innocent civilians and safeguard the implementation of ARCSS peace agreement as it is, playing with the cards of sovereignty and treason is a cheap attempt to dodge the genuine goals and objectives of such force. South Sudan is miserably off-track and has lost control and ability of driving herself back to safety and peace, hence, the best thing we can do to ourselves is not to indulge as usual in the same state of denial and the business of false pride and ego but to humbly welcome our regional and international friends to help save us from the evil of our own.

August 16, 2016
In a Nutshell

I bet things aren't alright in the Kiir & Co. ruling establishment and It seems like Beny Kiir is now concerned about himself more than the fate of those who has been running the show for him in the background and investing on his shortcomings, playing on his fears, boggling his mind with illusions or seductions of power and glory while they were busy robbing him from everything, his legacy, his rule, his reputation and the worst, his people and the country. Beny Kiir is about to open his eyes when his rule and legacy are almost over and here is the UN and International community are coming to protect the people of South Sudan from their own president and their own so-called national army, the SPLA.

Well, more troubles are on the way and the little left from Kiir & Co. reputation is now being internationally tarnished as the rapist soldiers from the so-called national army didn't even spare foreign women as well. Poor Beny Kiir.

Juba and Beny Kiir seem to be in complete shock about how things have reached the stage of international intervention, how the United Nation Security Council swiftly and overwhelmingly reached its decision of approving the intervention force with majority of eleven members and with only four members who have chosen to save the little they have with Juba by being absent and even with these four, nothing much of their absence indicate any of good will but to save some bloody businesses of oil contracts and arms dealings and which also made the arms embargo resolution a failure. Now, the rift within Kiir & Co. establishment started to surface and the Beny is trying to distant himself from the perpetrators of the bloody July 7th - 11th and its aftermath of summary execution of civilians and gang rape of women based on their ethnicity, massive looting to properties and businesses, to sum it up, the July 7th -11th event has proved that there isn't a government in control and those who are armed can just do anything they wanted.

Kiir & Co. are experiencing their first test with the international laws and they would do a grave miscalculation by applying their ego and defiance they have been using against Riek Machar with the United Nation and the international community. While Malong Awan, Kuol Manyang backed my JCE want to confront the foreign intervention, Beny Kiir is in limbo and emphasizing on the "Konkoch" strategy and he is seeing in the confrontation of the Intervention forces an immediate threat to his rule and sure end to his throne. Kiir also ordered the investigation on the clashes of July 7th-11th as well as the massive rape campaign on South Sudanese and foreign women and girls and which the UNMISS has documented and has solid evidence. But how far is the effect of the Gen.Taban factor in the sudden change in the mode and direction of the regime and in particular president Kiir's, is what we may need to know!

Of course. the Kiir & Co. want to prove that Riek Machar was the problem and hence a change in attitude and performance must follow such a claim and there must be improvement in government performance and policies and in which Gen. Taban is doing his best by offering his best advice and ideas directly to Kiir an approach that may create a conflict in policy and direction with that of JCE's. Well, in the light of Taban factor, we should expect some new political conspiracies and wrangling within the Kiir & Co. ruling establishment and that may lead to new political realities. Stay tuned.

August 17 , 2016
In a Nutshell

Dr. Riek Machar is waging a reforms war in his hideouts in Equatoria bushes, SG. Pagan Amum was seen demonstrating with hundreds of South Sudanese in New York calling for International Intervention, Dr. Lam Akol is yet to break his silence since his sudden resignation from TGoNU, Dr. Majok Agot is also in limbo somewhere in US and with some appearances here and there being interviewed about what should be done to save South Sudan from itself. Well, these are all pockets of opposition to Kiir failed rule and namely SPLM-IO, SPLM-FD and SPLM-DC turned DC. Since the bloody events of July, neither of these SPLM/A political or military factions is still intact, with some remained within TGoNU, declared alliance with Kiir and staged coup against their movements. A quick revisit to how the events of

December 2013 has unfolded and in which the main SPLM/A big bang explosion produced its many faces and shapes with the exception of the SPLM-DC of Dr. Lam Akol which its split was forced earlier when Mr. Akol was being accused as the lone rebel leader associated with Johnson Olouny armed faction before he "Olouny" was in with Kiir and out against Kiir to ally himself with SPLM/A-IO of Dr. Machar.

Upon their release from the Kiir's detention as a result of the aftermath fabricated coup and which Dr. Machar forces sacrificed thousands of its fighters to make their release possible, the SPLM-Former Detainees stopped short of joining Machar and they were either confused or reluctant to declare a way forward of their own neither decided to join Dr. Machar armed rebellion despite the later sacrifices for their release and hence denied to give a national political and military boost to SPLM/A-IO and which at that time being weaken through propaganda of being a Nuer movement when the political wrangling was still foggy and unclear. Nor did the former detainees were successful to form a viable political movement with any clear political agenda against or with Kiir nor with the SPLM/A-IO of Dr. Machar, however, they managed to be included as part of the peace process with a minimum role and subsequently as part of TGoNU.

Coming to the point, both the SPLM/A-IO, SPLM-FD and SPLM-DC turned DC are all in opposition against Kiir regime yet they failed from day one to formulate an effective national alliance being political or military that would serve as a broad national democratic front for change and reforms, uniting South Sudanese people from all walks of life and various different political affiliations to defeat Kiir and JCE tyranny regime. Strategically, this kind of political or military alliance could serve as a national majority base which Kiir can't either win against it neither politically or militarily, well, to our dismay, this has been not possible for the last three years and hence it have created an ill-fated, weak and exclusive opposition not being able to mobilize the masses of South Sudanese, nationally around a national agenda for change and reforms and which may be due to conflicted interests and the grudges of the past of our politicians of both aforementioned SPLM/A factions. To sum it up, they neither can unite nor can they defeat Kiir in their fragmented political or military factions, a dilemma.

However, if these fragmented opposition factions are dreaming of victory over Kiir tyranny regime then they must leave behind their selfish interests and past grudges and be born again out of their corrupted past with Kiir and formulate a political or military alliance to remove Kiir from power or force him to accept the needed fundamental change. Well, the question is whether such alliance is possible within a political movement that is characterized by selfishness and given Gen. Taban coup against his boss and in law Dr. Machar as a good example of such mistrust and how one would choose to advance his/her selfish interest on the expenses of public good and interest. How if the SPLM/A-IO leadership was firm and united behind Dr. Machar in pressing for the needed reforms and change until the end? What if the SPLM-FD upon release announced its support to SPLM/A-IO and joined its ranks to make a national movement? Couldn't things be different now? Well, this was far from being a reality.

Victory over Kiir won't happen without a solid, an inclusive national strategy and those who want to change the Kiir's regime must meet the prerequisites of any movement for change, they must unite and coordinates their efforts, work on a common purpose and have a national agenda and political program better than Kiir and his JCE. Otherwise, we should stop talking about removing Kiir from power.

August 17, 2016
In a Nutshell

In my previous "In a Nutshell" I reminded you that how ruthless Gen. Taban he may prove to be second to none but his first in command of the tribal militias Mathiang Annyor, Paul Malong. Launching his aggressive offensive ever against his former boss Dr. Riek Machar, the man has poured a fierce verbal hostile attack and threats of a grave scale to the person of Dr. Machar and of course his supporters in SPLM/A-IO and promising to crush them at all costs and through various means necessary, military offensive, assassinations through unknown gunmen, cluster bombs...etc.

Mr. Taban want to keep his new job at all costs and will do all the impossible to see himself succeeding. He is totally off topic and forgot in his power drunk mind that the problem of South Sudan has more to do with the established system in Juba and its unjust policies and actions. He simply forgot that the SPLM/A he claimed to represent is "In Opposition" and can't simply be added to Kiir "In Government" unless reforms or changes to tyrant governance system and unjust power sharing are made.

Replacing individuals and swapping positions between day and night isn't the solution to the problem of South Sudan because simply it doesn't address the underpinning factors and root causes of the conflict, while such a manipulative and opportunistic approach does fulfill those individuals' selfish interests, it doesn't do any good to the nation and country of South Sudan. In fact, it is a postponement of the core conflict and then to resurface at a different time, sooner or later.

Opportunists don't care and don't see far than their short noses and that's why they are the best tools of the tyrant governance systems to achieve their malicious goals in the long run. Gen. Taban is so power drunk to an extent that he forgot that the terms of peace he is violating and contradicting today was negotiated and spearheaded by himself as the lead negotiator.

Well, I understand that when political betrayers have started their heinous crimes of backstabbing their movements and objectives just for selfish gains, they in fact crossed to the other side of the river without a point of return. Gen. Taban and his followers has just done so and they are now part of Kiir establishment and have no credibility or right to talk about being an opposition or SPLM/A-IO.

Well, Kiir has been there with his established system, his JCE, his notorious security, unknown gunmen death squad, his tribal Mathiang Annyor, his high profile professionals think tanks framing for him his policies and political program...etc. but the SPLM/A-IO under the leadership of the able Dr. Machar was also there fighting these whole injustice crew and there is nothing of significant value Gat Nyakeak Lam can add except the political rhetoric and smearing propaganda.

August 20, 2016
In a Nutshell

Don't take it personal but if we have to make victory against Kiir & Co. tyranny and win the war against injustice and corrupt leadership then we must point clearly and bravely to where the destructive underlying factors resides in our leadership structure and strategies as well as within our society.

Not long ago that I have emphasized on the need to 're-engineer our social norms and values towards value addition and difference making, values that builds us up, empower us as we head towards the future and the unknown instead of scrambling with the old and the dysfunctional in 21st century. A thorough review and revision to our social norms and values system would do us a great service by identifying where the underlying causes of our socio-economic, political and cultural turmoil do originate and in the same time such a thorough review will help us knows and identify the strength aspects of the social values and cultural heritage.

Well, for instance political opportunism, political and financial corruption are probably and mostly linked to way a society or a portion of that society do thinks, lives its lifestyle, beliefs. What we see as betrayal and backstabbing here could be meant for smartness or cleverness there, embezzlement of public funds may not be considered a theft in some sections of our society.

One of the gravest mistake of Dr. Riek Machar is that he entrusted his life and the top affairs of SPLM/A-IO with people he knew nothing about nor their background or cultural drive neither their social norms or values. He entrusted mere political opportunists with his whole life and future of the movement. People who were quick to embrace him, sing his name loud, play on his fears and dreams. However, such a brand of people is in the political markets waiting for the higher bidder and with Mr. Kiir as president, someone who has the executive powers to appoints, elevates and promotes, the promises of Gat-Machar and the enforced decrees of Kiir have no comparison whatsoever only if Gat-Machar got it right by surrounding himself with true loyalists, principled followers, those who can't be sold or bought.

Too late anyway, the opportunists have sold the ARCSS in return of nothing since those jobs are Kiir's and he could withdraw them anytime to buy other political opportunists that are good, usable and useful for a different time when the time and usefulness of Al-Tabaneen expires. Riek Machar couldn't face all these hurdles and attempts of his life if he reads the history of people very well and accordingly entrust who with what. Well, he has a final chance anyway.

August 24, 2016
In a Nutshell

The SPLM/A-IO is a South Sudanese political movement that has a long-term mission and socio-economic, political and cultural programs meant to transform South Sudan, the nation and the country to the best it could, be it in terms of development, democratic aspirations, respect to human rights, and rule of law among others. We don't know exactly or can't predict precisely when it will reach to the seat of power given the lack of democratic transition of power in the hijacked country and the current harsh political realities locally, regionally and internationally that may or may not support such a quest. Neither we can predict that the movement will achieve that or not, within the lifetime of its current chairman Dr. Machar, however, the movement won't go to political extinction if its current Chairman has retired political activism or in his absence as our ill-wishers from the Kiir & Co. camp so wishes.

Just like any other political movements or parties with an

unpredictable lifetime, the SPLM/A-IO will follow the due process and as stipulated in its party charter and constitution should it be necessary to bring about the change in its leadership and please don't think it is going to be like the Kiir-sponsored coup that brought Al-Tabaneen to the stage of the current political sham and controversy but instead a real democratic process where the loyalist members of the SPLM/A-IO shall choose their next chairman in a fair, democratic process and norms as their current chairman Dr. Machar has engraved within the movement mindset and principles.

Does the SPLM/A-IO needs any blessings or approval from Kiir & Co. of what it is aiming to do to transform South Sudan to the best it could? Not at all, if they (Kiir & Co.) are matured political party (which they are not) they could have cooperated and worked hand in hand with other South Sudanese political forces to shape the way forward and transform our country to be the hub of democracy and prosperity in East Africa region if not in Africa as a whole but this is far from happening and instead they have transformed us into beggars for foods, scattered refugees and political asylees all around the world. With Riek Machar almost assassinated and escaped for his dear life, you can see Kuol Manyang today with 90% appearance and present in the SSBC and in all the delegations going out to sell the cheap coup against Dr. Machar. He is finally happy, he avenged his 1991 twice than he has expected using the full state machine and the entire national capabilities of the state to bring part of this nation to annihilation without the slightest shame and you still think we are a healthy nation, we are not!

This is the core problem of South Sudan; some South Sudanese thinks they have extra tails than the rest, dictating a monopoly rule and manipulative governance system through police/security state approach that has marginalized the rest and plunged the country into a tribal war and political chaos that has crippled the country economically and politically and destroyed the very social fabric in which the unity of the nation relays. Riek Machar, a South Sudanese politician that has sacrificed a lot for the sake of this nation and country at a time when his controversial haters, bias judges and all the Machar-phobia blind crows were just kids of yesterday who know nothing about the tribal internal politics of SPLM/A in the liberation days and which expelled many great patriots outward.

Nor the problem of South Sudan is Dr. Machar and if he has to retire politics today, the Kiir & Co. regime won't change an inch in its monopoly nor in its tyranny or its bloodiest police/security state approach but all they will do is to find another scapegoat and pretext to justify their cling on power and manipulate the national resources and capabilities of the state for their selfish and clannish interests. Nor the problem of South Sudan is the Nuer and sooner or later a national front of South Sudanese opposition forces will emerge with a national agenda to uproot the tyranny regime once and for all and at all costs and no matter how long it will take.

The SPLM/A-IO is here to stay in the forefront of that national opposition alliance and those who thinks they still have a political or diplomatic card to play with the Kiir & Co. they haven't learned a thing. Talking Kiir to peace is absolutely over, not an option at all. Ayieth.

September 5, 2016
In a Nutshell

So how did the UNSC diplomats got the hard stuff into the brains of the stone-headed government of Kiir Mayar and made them melt their utter defiance and arrogance in a matter of days and not only that but softly forced them to shamelessly swallowed their outburst and tempered statement "We won't accept even a single soldier". Well, now they are accepting not only "single soldier" but 4,000 soldiers, Ironic isn't it? I have seen the pictures of Makuei Lueth laughing so hard and chatting with UNMISS's boss and one would still wonder where does this man get the heart and the guts to laugh in such a way in a land where it is all skulls and skeletons of their own making? Sad indeed!

Whether it is a "Protection or Intervention force" this hasn't changed the number of the 4000 soldiers stated from the first day nor it did prevent their sure coming and so what the hell was all this noise about the so claimed sovereignty and foreign invasion? Nor does it make sense that the Kiir regime was all furious about "Intervention force" but finally consented to the "Protection force" of the foreign troops to come and protect the South Sudanese people from their own government "if it is really still their government and not their killer" and they wouldn't even ask themselves or the UN diplomats this simple question: You want to protect who from who?

Well, the answer is here: protecting the South Sudanese people from their own so-called national government and from their own so-called national army, since the two are no longer constitute a national government or national army respectively and this isn't a baseless claim rather than it is a true statement backed by a well-documented systematic power abuse, human rights violations and grave atrocities from either the Kiir's government and his tribal militias. Most of the massacres and grave atrocities committed and still being committed by Kiir regime were and still ethnic-based whether in Greater Upper Nile, Greater Equatoria or against Fertit and Jurchen tribes in Wau and the UNSC is not acting out of the blue but has a solid evidence and well-documented records of grave atrocities that even Kiir himself won't believe it is from his own Mathiang Annyor making.

The need for a national army and the necessity of overhauling all the tribal security organs is paramount to South Sudan peace and stability. This won't be possible but through the ARCISS agreement that the Al-Tabaneen have betrayed and sold out cheaply and with nothing in return but useless and temporary positions of FVP and Petroleum. The current Kuol-Malong tribal militias Mathiang Annyor can't fit to be called or regarded a national army in any form possible leave along their lengthy records of ethnic-based atrocities since the eruption of this war. Al-Tabaneen can't claim that they are implementing the ARCISS or will do so since they are but "Yes Stooges" that won't even say "NO" to anything coming from Kiir & JCE and a month of their own "TGoNU" with Kiir has already shown that as we haven't heard anything about the 28 states or any of the other pressing issues but the usual rhetoric of Riek Machar did this, Riek Machar did that, Pathetic enough!

Well, make no mistake about it, the ARCISS is here to stay and has its defenders, its advocates and those who are ready to die for its implementation in letter and spirit. It is an agreement meant to change this country and its nation for better and hence it can't be sold just for few meaningless positions that won't last longer than Kiir himself. Kiir positions are no permanent, he changes them as he changes his shoes and shirts and accordingly the fate of this country rely on the ARCISS and not on individuals' selfish interests. The SPLM/A-IO under the leadership of Dr. Riek Machar and in alliance with the rest of opposition forces in this country shall either press for the full implementation of the ARCISS or a total regime change. It is not over yet and the regional protection force is not here out of the blue, the UN surely knows that hard times are still ahead for this country and its nation.

September 13, 2016
In a Nutshell

Beny Kiir is a bank to so many people within South Sudan
and without regardless whether he has transformed his
country to the museum of skulls and skeletons of his dead
nation or an open house of corruption, where every
corrupt soul grabs freely, Beny Kiir will still have the loud
drummers and skilled dancers, dancing and singing loudly;
"long live Beny Kiir, keep them cash coming, let it rains"
and If you dare to cut Beny Kiir rule short, then you have
cut our cash short too and this is a crime in Kiir's country
punishable by death through the unknown gunmen death
squad.

The uproar caused by the Sentry report released yesterday
of who has embezzled what of $$$ billions reminds me
with the same uproar caused by AU report on the genesis
of the Juba massacres and the grave atrocities committed
on the thousands of innocent South Sudanese around the
country and particularly in Juba, Bentiu, Malakal and Wau
and before the slaughter reached the depth of Equatoria
region. So you may ask what difference did the AU report
on the bloody massacres and the grave atrocities on
innocent South Sudanese ever made that the Sentry report
on the grand theft of public money will ever make? I bet if
anyone still talk about the AU report now and so is the
Sentry report sooner than later.

I wish the West understands how Africa does functions
and operates and particularly those countries controlled by
rogue regimes and dictatorships and where public opinions
or popular votes don't make any difference since there is
no public accountability through fair democratic elections
where the people can vote-out corrupt and incompetent

leaders and freely vote-in better leaders. But in rogue regimes such as ours, it is all a one man show, the president that may rule indefinitely until he is no more, supported and defended by his henchmen and corrupt entourage. he could also be succeeded by his son or one of his immediate corrupt hire and where the cycle goes on for generation and who will remember what and who after 100 years. Chances are rare to find a brave and informed nation that don't submit to dictators or their corrupt money and particularly in Africa.

You shouldn't be surprised by either the AU or the yesterday Sentry report. Simply because, imagine a man who own the keys of the country banks, the fate of his innocent people, the keys of prisons and the most the blessings and condemnations in an absolute power unopposed whatsoever and imagine that man to be a king of corruption and the corrupts, the chief of the unknown gunmen and the supreme commander of genocidal army. Just imagine. It must be a sure hell kind of country and where killing of the citizens and looting of the public money must be the order of the day and this has been the South Sudan of Kiir Mayar since 2005 up to the present. I mean the leadership should be adhered to heavenly values that give regards to life and high values of honesty and credibility but when it is the opposite then expect a constant nightmare on earth.

Don't panics yet because the worst is still to come, with Kiir Mayar regime being enabled by the corrupt region and supported by misinformed international figures, the killing and the looting of South Sudan would stop until it is no more. The regime now has mostly sold the oil reserves in secret deals with rogue countries and businesses in forms of cash loans to survive on after they managed their economy to bankruptcy, other loans in form of heavy weapons and the latest was few days ago which rewarded the regime with two fighting jets to be used against its own people, to shut-off the voices that are calling for change of the killer and thief regime, weapons that strengthen its killings and looting powers even further. So you wonder how this world operates, giving us reports and giving the killer and the thief, deadly weapons.

While such reports as AU and Sentry may hurt the regime internationally in some cases, it won't change the regime tight grip on power or its police/security state approach and in fact, the regime will just lose her mind even more. In a nutshell, the West must be serious enough with the regime of South Sudan by imposing arms embargo, support the ARCISS agreement implementation and of course I don't mean the Al-Tabaneen latest political gambling but the real and serious one led by Dr. Machar otherwise it needs to stop reporting to us about Killing and theft that we knew they are the order of the day since 2005 until now. Thank you, George Clooney and Dan Chadile, fixing Africa is a no joke.

September 21, 2016
In a Nutshell

The current political wrangling between those who defected with Gen. Taban to Kiir's camp and those who remained loyal to the leadership of Dr. Machar is not about the position of First Vice President (FVP) allocated by the ARCISS agreement to the SPLM/A-IO or neither it is about Dr. Reik Machar in person as the defectors been claiming in justifying their sellout of the agreement in return for nothing but selfish gains as Ministers, MPs and Advisors and so on. or as they are justifying their shameful backstabbing to the SPLM/A-IO movement and the struggle of South Sudanese people throughout the bloody three years' war (2013 -2016). Those who remained loyal to the leadership of Dr. Machar have done so because there was never a reason that should warrant a drastic change in the leadership of the movement while the main objective was the implementation of the agreement. The main concern here is the peace agreement since it is the program for change and reforms, the cornerstone that a new South Sudan could be realized, gradually but surely, if implemented fully.

The agreement is what should bend both parties' signatories to the agreement to enable the reforms agreed upon and throughout the projected period of the implementation until the presumed elections in 2018. The agreement is the only safeguard that will enable a creation of new national army that should be drawn from all diverse tribes of South Sudan, an army that is trained professionally on what its national role should be, an army that is guided by professionalism, high standards of ethics and values, an army that will be the real defense shield of South Sudanese unity, peace and stability and not the other way around as we have seen in both factions of the SPLM/A; SPLA-IG and SPLM-IO. This is a very fundamental concern since what is regarded now as a national army is far from being so in all aspects of nationalism and representation of the 64 tribes of South Sudan, neither in its command and control structure nor in its manpower ranks and files.

Additionally, if honored and implemented, the agreement would be the facilitator of a new national security organ that its duty is to secure and not terrorize the citizen, a national security that is above manipulation and exploitation of any sort and not as we have seen it being manipulated to eliminate tribal, personal and political opponents or its vast powers being used to terrorize the ordinary citizens and seizure of their properties. Mr. Taban and Co. have defected single-handedly and without any military unit of SPLM/A-IO leave alone a full battalion, hence what will he integrate? Does he think the Mathiang Annyor tribal militias should be the South Sudan national army or would he enact the reforms engraved in the agreement with support of these Malong-Kuol tribal militias who also the very anti-agreement? It just doesn't add up ya Tabaneen and admit it, there is no agreement here that's being implemented.

On the same note, the hijacked FVP, the ministers, the advisors and all the positions down the line, are here because of the agreement, they are part of the power sharing provided and agreed upon through the agreement, they are, though provided, respected and protected through and by the agreement respectively. That's, the positions will not be honored in the long run as they are unsustainable by any secured and bending agreement, if you have nullified the agreement, the positions, and all the power-sharing deals, are accordingly nullified as well. Hence, Mr. Taban & Co. are temporarily standing on a carpet that may be pulled by Kiir at any time of his choosing and they would have no power to say a word or reject such a move.

While the Al-Tabaneen are saying they are implementing the agreement as SPLM/A-IO, the question is how is that when they have 99.99% of the SPLM/A-IO military and political base all but not with them but in fact against them? What will they do if Kiir fire them in two or three months? How would they protest or defend the agreement or says their positions? Above all, how would they implement the peace agreement without a political and military backing from the people who have fought the war and sacrificed the precious for the last three years and are ready to do so again and again in case Mr. Salva decided not to honor the agreement? Would they beg Kiir to implement the various institutional and governance reforms recommended by the agreement? If so, what did they achieve with that strategy since the bloody July of their Hotel coup up to the present? Did Kiir nullify any of his infamous decrees and particularly the drastic 36/2015 decree of the 28 states? Did the thousands of IDPs in UNMISS finally got convinced that their own country and the government is safer and better than the UN and its many camps around the country? If the answers to those questions is No, then this isn't the peace nor is the solution to the conflict in our country and we shouldn't deceive ourselves, it is better for Al-Tabaneen to admit their own selfish course that won't benefit the country and the nation of South Sudan and for Juba to reclaim its lost sanity and sobriety.

Only fools think the international community has abandoned the ARCISS peace agreement and finally has yielded to the unilateral solution of Kiir & Co. No, they haven't done so nor they are ignorant of who the fake SPLM/A-IO is and who is the real one or the scenario that led to the replacement of the legitimate FVP Dr. Reik Machar. In fact, the recent Sentry report and the US senate hearing should worry both Kiir & Co. as well as their puppets, the Taban & Co. The world knows by details what is in fact, happening in secret corridors of Kiir regime and accordingly they must be ready for more unpleasant surprises in the not too far future.

The political naive thinks that by exiling Dr. Reik Machar and isolating him from politics, all South Sudan problems will be gone overnight. That's not true leave alone that it is a childish thinking. The origin of all South Sudan problems is Kiir leadership that has created all this untold mess and failures, the country is a big prison now, people are living in fears and hunger. Free speech, human rights and civil liberties are long gone, press freedom is no more, unknown gunmen are finishing the dissent voices, the economic situation is in upheaval and turmoil, foreign relations with most of the world are at worse shape and the insecurity has forced millions of South Sudanese to flee the country, Abyei is a gone case, the social fabric of this nation is ultimately destroyed and the country is so divided than ever. Someone need to tell me where Kiir leadership did best throughout his 11 years' rule? Kiir and Co. are here because they have been scapegoating Dr. Machar and nearly in every failure of their own and if Machar has to choose silence and exile for only one year, you will see how Kiir regime fall in disarray at no time.

October 3 2016
In a Nutshell

Even if Kiir re-invented himself through Gen Taban, winning the trust and financial support from the international community would be nearly impossible. Taban will be touring the world talking about unrealistic peace and of course, the war and blame it all on Riek Machar but this seems to be only helping him on why he is here and not Riek Machar but he must not be content with that simply because the world knows very well that when you say Riek Machar, you just don't mean the individual Riek Machar rather than a 100,000 of armed forces and more than half of the country supporting him in his bid to change the rogue regime of Kiir & JCE.

The International community would be foolish enough to spend a dime sponsoring Taban's bid of stabilizing an economy of an ongoing war or insecurity that its factors are still active and counting. There is more to the quest of stabilizing South Sudan economically and in terms of insecurity, this includes the need to deal with the real partners of the conflict. If you need real peace, you make peace with your real enemies and not with people who have nothing with the conflict, that will be a deception to oneself and this is exactly what the Juba regime been doing to itself, celebrating its own deception in what it called peace with SPLM/A-IO-Hotel after they thought they have vaporized the real SPLM/A-IO. However, as a matter of fact, the conflict is still here and active, shutting down all the economic activities in the country and forcing people out of the country on daily basis and hence, how can you even talk about stabilizing the economy or the security situation? The International community has no money to waste on unrealistic missions.

With Riek declaration of war, now Kiir will come back to face again the reality he refused in July and as always been trying to avoid and this time, he might not be given any benefit of the doubts, neither through Dr. Machar's goodwill nor through any fake games of JMEC, IGAD or Troika. War is a reality, if it is not Riek Machar, Lam Akol will do it, if not Lam, the Equatorians, Murle and Fretit are here. the propaganda that war was a Nuer-Dinka war is already a proven lie. This is a national dilemma caused by Mr. Kiir's weak leadership. The International community knows very well that war is not over yet and you can see why they are insisting on the deployment of their 4000 protection force. Hence, they would spend $$$$ only on this force or on humanitarian assistance which goes directly to NGOs and not Kiir's regime. They know that Mr. Taban and Co. are not realistic partners in the decision of making peace or war, they have nothing but words and political gambling and the blame game on Riek Machar but they have no army nor the necessary political base that can make the war come to a halt.

New political realities will emerge as the war resume, those who has an army on the ground whether in SPLM/A-IO or IG will shape those realities and since Mr. Taban doesn't have that heavy weight kind of alliance to Kiir as

Monytuel brothers of Bull Nuer, it is likely that he might be dumped and be replaced. Well, his chances are that he secures an alliance with the Monytuels and others but why he should be given the lead to that alliance and not the Monytuels? That's another challenge and hence, rejection of such an alliance could be his.

October 4, 2016
In a Nutshell

I wish, me and you, to be the last frontier that wouldn't be able to be confused or convinced by the Al-Tabaneen operators and as they embark on their many tactics and many changing faces, recruiting, confusing and forging their way through and in a bid to dismantle the remaining faithfuls of the SPLM/A-IO. One of the shocking discoveries after the defection of Mr. Taban and Mr. Lol Gatkuoth and the rest of their crew is the realization of the fact that not everyone who screams loud Viva IO or Viva Riek Machar is either a genuine member of SPLM/A-IO nor who shed tears on the Nuer 2013 massacres or who enthusiastically call for Nuer Ayeith is a genuine member of the Nuer community and having the real interest of the Nuer people of South Sudan. There is more to loyalty and commitment to any movement or community, it can be traced, it can be proven and cross or double-checked using many factors and tests, something the Chairman Reik Machar has neglected and then he was completely surrounded with people of that sort, confusing him and selling him at the same time and until the straw broke the Camel's back in the last bloody July incidents, sadly.

The ranks and file of both SPLM/A-IO and the Nuer Community are widely infested with people that are doing the enormous harms to both entities and it is sad to say that the Nuer massacre of 2013 may have been planned with the help of some Nuer sons or daughters in

157

collaboration with Kiir & JCE and not to forget the early stages of these massacres where it all started with Lou Nuer being massacred nearly on daily basis. It sounds that some Nuer while faking Nuer unity and Nuer interest, they are allying themselves with the same regime they are portraying to us as an enemy of the Nuer in order to advance their own interests and climb the ladder to power and national politics. Well, we are not stupid or fools as they may have thought or been thinking, Oops, only that we thought we were all genuine and honest in the call for Nuer unity, both in Ethiopia and South Sudan, and that we should advance the interest of the Nuer people in these two sisterly countries and it is never that we don't know that even though we are all Nuer albeit citizens of two different countries and where rights and privileges could also vary accordingly and hence a need to know who is who or who occupy what is needed in both SPLM/A-IO and the Nuer community. This can help in determining who is here to advance the real cause of our people and who is here just to manipulate the name of the Nuer in order to advance his/her own or group interest. I really think there is a need for the Nuer people to double check when it comes to throwing their support at every new defector or those smart chameleons who seem to know what to use to blindfold them in order to solicit support.

The politics we are seeing is becoming the politics of "Chi-nya-betrayer" joining Taban or "Chi-nya-loyalist" staying with Riek just to advance their clan interests while the Nuer collective interest is no more a cause. This is dangerous approach and doesn't benefit but only selfish individuals who are pursuing this kind of fragmentation politics and it is the beginning of the death of the Nuer as a powerful tribe both in politics and social platforms of South Sudan and accordingly, it must be resisted by all means necessary and its beneficiaries and champions held accountable. Conquer to rule is a very effective strategy and no one should reminds us about that as it all succeeded in both old Sudan and Africa and it is unfortunate that even though those who have been struggling to unchain and liberate themselves from the domination and servitude of those who conquered and dominated them, came finally to apply the same method on their new portrayed second class citizens or enemies and this is what is destroying South Sudan at the moment, a miserable contradiction to the past and the present. Accordingly, a reality check is all needed within the SPLM/A-IO or the Nuer Community.

October 6, 2016
In a Nutshell

You may wonder and ask if there is any peace implementation going on right now under SPLM/A-Hotel aka Al-Tabaneen? if so, what has been implemented so far? Well, absolutely nothing since their takeover in the bloody July hotel coup. Nevertheless, rumors have it that when Gen. Taban tried to convince Gen. Kiir to overhaul and nullified the 28 states decree at least to save some wet on his well dried and drained face and boost his morale amidst the massive rejection and reaction from the SPLM/A-IO loyalists at national level and the Nuer community in particular, labeling him as a traitor and backstabber to the cause of the struggling South Sudanese people against Kiir-JCE tyranny.

Apparently, when the news of Mr. Taban asking Kiir to nullify the 28 states decree reached the JCE and the corridors of power in the ruling establishment, the reaction was swift and the JCE and its many political tribal affiliates angrily resolved to replace Gen. Taban with governor Joseph Monytuel if he insisted further on issue of the 28 states and accordingly a new policy and conspiracy was enacted encouraging the Monytuels to ask for replacement of Taban and to demand to have the FVP as theirs since they have been one of president Kiir powerful political and military ally who stood by him despite the fact that he was slaughtering their own Nuer people.

In the wake of his learning about such news, Gen. Taban has no other alternative but to stop pressing on the issue of 28 states and not only that but he may never ask Kiir to change or nullify any of his infamous decrees again. That's, Taban will refrain from any future adventures of attempting to challenge any decrees or any plans from Mr. Kiir or JCE as he may risk getting fired or replaced with the Monytuels at any time and since Gen. Taban can't even think about returning to Riek Machar camp, nor can he press for any fundamental changes in the Kiir-JCE rogue regime fearing replacement, Mr. Taban is here to implement the Kiir-JCE plans and policies, fully and unopposed, fulfilling and fitting the good and patriotic Nuer according to JCE perception.

Well, such a scenario is an attempt to answer your (ours) wonders whether there is going to be really "a peace implementation" as we and the rest of the world are being deceived by Al-Tabaneen that they are here to implement the peace agreement, the fact is, you can't serve two masters in this situation, if you love your FVP or the Petroleum minister positions to an extent that you can't give them up, then for sure you can't serve the second master the " peace implementation" and since your boss is against the very "peace implementation" then it will be a hit of joke to tell us that you will dare even to ask your boss. You will get fired and replaced. Case close.

Accordingly, there is no peace to be implemented by Al-Tabaneen and this is the very reason why people of this country may return to war which is never a good option but those who have dismantled the peace agreement did make the return to war, a reality. They have enabled the war by destroying the peace but their tongues and propaganda machines are louder than their true intents, appointing themselves in the place of the SPLM/A-IO and claiming to implement the peace agreement and as time passes, their true color and objective, is but being exposed on daily basis and clearer than ever. They are in dilemma, they can't rejoin the true patriotic SPLM/A-IO neither they can implement a rat with Kiir, in fact, they should continue to pray that Kiir won't dump them and slaughter them like chicken, and it is about time.

October 8, 2016
In a Nutshell

The South Sudanese people are paying a heavy price because of the tribal policies of the failed leadership in Juba. They are the fuel of this power struggle war that's being waged under the pretext of tribal war and they are the one dying on a daily basis whether directly in the battlefields or indirectly from the various war-related causes, be it hunger or diseases. Undoubtedly, South Sudanese are divided than ever and our social fabric that was beautifully woven by century-long tribal intermarriages and kinships is but no more. Those who were born by the late 60s and early 70s know very well how the South Sudanese lived side by side as one nation and co-existed in a rare peace and harmony even though we were under North Sudan domination and rule that uses the "divide-to-rule" policy most often, promoting this tribe to the level of 'Master" and demoting that tribe to the level of "Slave" or as they so wish in their systematic policies of domination.

In early 80s, and when 1st field Marshal, late Jafaar Nemeri, the then president of Sudan shifted its blessings and policies towards Equatorians giving them vice presidency in the Sudan central government and the South semi-autonomous regional government which to best of my memory were occupied by "Jienga" and upon the official kick-off of Kokora which was the policy sustained by the North and its objective was to deepen the divide of South Sudan and destroy the persisting strong unity. However, and from Equatorians narratives and perspectives, the Kokora was a reactive policy, triggered by the Jienga domination to the semi-autonomous South regional government, it is said that the nepotism and tribal domination to some ministries and government departments could have reached 90% of one ethnicity dominating all the jobs, from the minister down to the gateman.

Land grabbing and discrimination in housing was another factor that has encouraged the Equatorians to adopt the policy of Kokora. With power and money concentrated in the hands of Jienga, the Equatorians found themselves not only being marginalized in the government but worse than that, they were losing their land, houses, and dignity altogether. One of incident that I still freshly remember in the wake of Kokora and when everyone was moving back to their own state of origin, people of Malakal to Malakal and those of Wau to Wau, is a story of man who have cut all the beautiful trees he planted in his house while in his host state (Malakal) because he is moving back to his mother-state. This was because of Jalaba of North Sudan as we all be singing before the independence.

Then what? After the independence and under the very government of the movement (SPLM/A) and the people who have led the liberation war and promised us a dawn and future that will be better 100 times than the one we had patiently endured and suffered for decades and liberated ourselves from with a very heavy price of 3 million precious souls. In its 11 years of rule, the SPLM/A, the leadership composed mainly from those who founded and led the movement from its very inception, has miserably and collectively failed the people of South Sudan. In its failure, it failed also to admit that it has failed to lead the country and instead they turned inward, destroying the nation, by inciting acute and negative tribalism and using tribes against tribes, just to stay in power. In my previous "In a Nutshell" writings I have warned many times of the consequences of such tribal policies because, in the long run, it destroys the very nation we all call ours, however, with the new found power and wealth, our leaders seem to be so blind to read the dire consequences and implications of such policies and they have just chosen instead to go deep into the abyss.

Now that the Kokora is about to remerge, not only in Equatoria but this time it seems it is all South Sudan that is in it, our people are killing each other everywhere, innocent people whose Juba policies pitted and made enemies and who have nothing to gain in such war but their sure demise. We are so divided on tribal line and this is proved by the fact that in some areas within South Sudan, you will not find a person of some tribes deemed enemy or persona non grata, a very sad reality indeed; this wasn't the way South Sudan was in late 60s and until 1980. All in all, this political mess and failure reminds me that some people who went to bush in 1982 and after what they call a dishonor to Addis Ababa agreement didn't really mean to liberate South Sudan from the domination of North Sudan and build a one nation, one country rather than to restore a lost throne and return us to the domination of Jienga and subsequently to another Kokora, such a policy is a reality of the day and it is still manifesting. Well, the political turmoil we are in, falsify the very theory of "we are born to rule" and "we have liberated you" and as soon as we abandoned such wrong concepts, that will be the beginning of the birth of a great nation, South Sudan. May God save South Sudan from the evil of itself and others.

October 14. 2016
In a Nutshell

The question the president should ask himself is: what crime(s) he committed to the people who are so bitter on him to an extent they wished him the worst, his rumored death? If he tried to answer that question, the president will refresh his mind about the horrors these people have lived and experienced in the hands of his many killing tools, the tribal army, the security organs or the unknown gunmen throughout his 11 years of bloody rule. Apart from the 2013 Nuer massacres, let us take for example the way SPLM/A-IO officers George and Domach were murdered in cold blood on July 7th, 2016 by Kiir NSS and their bodies dumped in such heartless way and like they have no children, families, and relatives that has been hurt so much by their brutal death. Well, what would the families and relatives and children of these victims would wish to the president? Absolutely not some sweet candies.

Well, until the rumored death of the president broke the camel's back and made some people for the first time to know that there is a lot of death in South Sudan and that death is truly a painful lost, unfortunately death has been the norm and the song of the day in South Sudan from 2005 to present and the South Sudanese mortality rate from 2005 - 2016 caused by various insecurity related factors have more than doubled but no one was even giving it a damn.

Well, another example was in the bloody July, when the SPLM/A-IO small protection unit were being rained upon by non-stop spray of bullets from land and air and anyone who have witnessed that or saw the video, would not think that those who are being deliberately massacred are South Sudanese and their lives matters too at least to their children and families but alas no one ever pretended to shed even some crocodile tears leave alone condemning such an evil trend but all were in celebratory mode of the rumored death of Riek Machar, Gen. Gatwech Dual, Gen. Koang Chuol Ranley, slaughtering whole goats and dancing around whiskey bottles declaring finally "we got him" "the head of Riek Machar" and as their Ambassador Gordon Buay announced in his Facebook page that they have the heads of IO top generals. In fact, Juba and their Facebook fans been celebrating the rumored death of Riek Machar for nearly one month until he surfaced victoriously, alive and kicking in Congo.

There are reasons why nations loves their leaders and presidents to an extent they were almost worshiping them and devastated if they are no more. If you look at all these great countries of the world, they weren't built to such greatness but through leaders who, with wisdom, reasoning and sacrifices managed to uplift their nations and countries to world class standards in development, peace and security. These achievements didn't just come from the sky, but they were through a sound leadership of some iconic men and women who devoted it all for the sake of their people. In contrary, some countries and nations have almost disappeared from the map of the world and became the pain to the world's security and stability because of failed leaders and leadership.

The president is here to make the lives of his people worth a value and not seeing them dies on daily basis like worthless flies, he is here to first protect them from any harm, internally and externally, and work tirelessly to uplift their living standards through sound socio-economic and political policies but what has been happening since 2005 has been indeed the opposite. Mr. Kiir and his administration should make a bit of statistics about the death tolls of South Sudanese since 2005 until present and compare them with the day we were united with North Sudan. It is a complete tragedy but he is the least to dare to know and care.

Mr. President has unparalleled powers to make South Sudan a great country in all aspects if he got a program of actions based on a clear vision of what he wants South Sudan to be and look like. I rarely noticed him talking about how can he fix the economy, achieve prosperity and provide security all around the country and not Juba alone but his talk mainly been about Riek Machar and his many imaginary enemies. Some people say the man is good at heart, kind and so on but this doesn't really make him a good president, a good president is one who translates this kindness and care to realities, build hospitals for the sick, schools for future generations, clean water, and electricity for his people…etc. He has powers to transform this country to the best it could, unfortunately, it seems those powers has been misused, abused and instead are being used to kill, rob and destroy the very people of South Sudan he wants to lead for the rest of his life but not in a good way. No one in his right mind and psychological health can ever wish a death to a human being unless there is a strong reason to that. Well, it is up to the president to find it out and fix it and my fears is that it may be too late.

October 15, 2016
In a Nutshell

I never cast a single doubt that the SPLM/A-IO is the tool for change and transformation of South Sudan to a better country and nation despite the hurdles and the obstacles that it will encounter along the way. The old mindset that has been controlling the SPLM/A as a movement and as a government of the day and that is wearing a beautiful fake nationalism but in fact, deep there, is but a group of few opportunists using tribalism as a support system. This old mindset will resist the needed transformation and change by all means and propaganda machine it has at its disposal, setting a stiff resistance to protect its narrow interests and gains in which its established rogue system, has been and still, sustaining and supporting ever since.

In its march and socio-economic, political and cultural transformation bid, the SPLM/A-IO could experience all sorts of setbacks, it will be backstabbed by the political opportunism and those of selfish interests, there will be defectors, betrayers and sabotages of all forms that will try to destroy it from within, selling it all cheap for selfish interests, those who in fact pretended to champion the national cause for change and interest but in fact are wolves in sheep clothes, looking and advancing their interests and quest for personal, tribal or clannish political power. The SPLM/A-IO, will have its internal and external doubting Thomases, constantly doubting its keenness, honesty, abilities and willingness to attain and form an inclusive and national country for people of South Sudan based on an inclusive national constitution, an inclusive system of governance, fair distribution of power and resources among the people of South Sudan and until they see it, they won't believe it.

The SPLM/A-IO as it marches on daily basis to be an inclusive national movement and the tool for change and transformation for a better South Sudan can't deny that huge sacrifices and work are needed to make the South Sudanese dream a reality neither this dream cannot be realized without a sound and effective leadership supported by its faithful masses. It is better that we skip the hangovers called for by the opportunists who either lack the needed capacity or vision to foresee the consequences and implications of bad peace or either received rewards from the rogue system in form of positions or financial bribes and then decided to stop the march towards the final glorious destination of our nation and country in the name of fake peace. Bad peace is a postponement of war, yet to be fought in another time, a time when the oppressors are even stronger and hence the South Sudanese people shall never cease the march and the struggle for an everlasting real peace and a stable country and nation.

Dr. Machar, the founder of the SPLM/A-IO and with a life and legacy that reflects all the struggle against the tribal mindset within the SPLM/A, is a living history of such struggle. I have no doubt that, Dr. Machar and his faithful colleagues within the SPLM/A-IO will deliver the new South Sudan, and if not in their lifetime, the next generations will keep the march and the legacy until victory.

October 18, 2016
In a Nutshell

Thank God and the gallant forces of the SPLM/A-IO who protected Dr. Riek Machar during the last bloody July ordeal netted and woven carefully by Kiir-JCE ruling clique and their greedy allies in the region and the world. July of 2016 has also reminded me of the sad July of 2005 when Dr. Garang life was cut short in a time he was about to embark on the second phase of liberation of his people and translate his vision into reality hadn't been the crash of his plane, South Sudan could be by now the promising leader of East Africa region economically and politically as well. July also is the month South Sudan referendum was conducted and which has led as well to our glorious Independence on July 9th, 2005. So why is July and what July got to do with South Sudan fate and destiny, its troubled leaders' lives and all the suspected conspirators behind its drastic events including the man in the seat of power in J1, his JCE or the driver minds who once hated Dr. Garang to death or is the whole thing a mere coincidence. Well, the truth hasn't been buried this time and around in July 2016 unlike in July 2005 death of Dr. Garang and whatever they have discussed in his last meeting with Museveni, the president of Uganda before he boarded that ill-fated hilocaptor.

Dr. Machar is here very much alive and in his many recent interviews by many world media channel outlets, he started narrating the facts and details of what exactly happened in July, both in J1 Kiir Palace and after they have been forced out to the jungles of Equatoria under a heavy attack, on the land and on the air, aided by sophisticated drone surveillance and spy technologies. They have been pursued day and night for 40 days until he decided to exit through Congo, to seek medical attention and to let the world know of the exact events that took place in the corridors of Kiir's Palace otherwise he could have stayed safely within South Sudan territories and under the protection of his gallant forces. The importance of Dr. Machar testimony has been necessitated by the fact that the conspiracy which almost cost him his life, was quickly and swiftly adopted as a reality and particularly when it is being presented as an internal SPLM/A-IO leadership rift and replacement in which both JMEC, IGAD, Troika, the region, and the world has shown willingness to buy. So there were two parallel events taking place, Dr. Machar being forced out and at a point of a gun being made absent and at the same time being replaced due to "this forced absenteeism" by a conspirator from his own SPLM/A-IO namely Gen. Taban Deng Gai. Well, those who are interested in knowing the truth and the details of the last bloody July ordeal should access those voice and video interviews. The funniest part of this whole ordeal is the pistol part, a lie which has reduced the supposed to be statesmen, to some sort of street boys, kids' behaviors and cowboys' storytellers. Dr. Machar has strongly dismissed it as a "Big Lie"

The question to Kiir and his bloody company is of course; why wasting South Sudanese people lives, resources and destroying the country yet to abrogate the expensive peace agreement reached to put that suffering to rest once and for all? Even the Mathiang Anyor who are dying for Kiir, Manyang and Malong's war, they have lives and future to worry about too. The fact is, from 2013 -2016, Kiir and Co. has taken the SPLM/A-IO, IGAD, AU, Troika for a ride of something they haven't intended to do, the quest for a permanent political settlement for the many pending and serious issues in the foundation of the new nascent nation, constitutional issues, institutional issues, governance, power and resources sharing, state structural issues and many more and which the new independent country is in so much need to address in order to avoid falling into persisting conflicts of all sorts. The 2013 political turmoil which ended with bloody ethnics' massacres was not a product of chance but its causes lies deep within the unhealthy political environment the ruling party SPLM has been operating at since the liberation days. Most of the attempts to inject a form of nationalism and democratic institutions into the movement and the state were stiffly resisted and deemed to failure, however, the conflict underpinnings were and still alive and driving South Sudan to be the troubled and unstable country of today.

Had the IGAD peace agreement of August 2015 been implemented without violations accumulated in July, 2016 and hadn't the Kiir & CO decided to save their ego and narrow interests first rather than the South Sudanese people interests in peace, economic development, security and political stability then where would we be now? South Sudan could by now on the course of rebuilding, reconciliation and healing, something the war and insecurity business moguls wouldn't buy. Dr. Machar is here to stay, no one has a right to ban him from politics, nor will he accept intimidations and pressure to leave his people's cause unfinished. He is a man of peace but should you choose the war, he and his people will defend themselves to the last man standing.

October 21, 2016
In a Nutshell

Do we have the good intentions and objectives in this notion of us Africans all rushing to control our governments? Well, we will be lucky if we get the type of president John Magufuli of Tanzania but I believe the majority of us are not in for good reasons. Obviously because in tribally structured societies of African nature such as ours in South Sudan, the political and social competition is not channeled by the leadership toward a good purpose, a national one. That's they are likely not competing to advance their national and common interests as a nation but competing to advance their tribal interests, competing to annihilate and destroy themselves, rushing to control and use the 'national government" to suppress other, manipulating the "national capabilities and resources of the state to empower and enrich their own, clans and tribes but the hell is when the head of the state or the leadership of the country is complicit in this, that's for sure the sure end (case of Kiir & JCE). I have been telling you guys that the whole problem is in "J1" not because the one that occupying that palace is your uncle and not mine but because the 'J1" should be the brain of the nation and where all the good things are planned, designed and ordered to be implemented top-down but unfortunately, the "J1" became the "demise" of the nation, where all the bad spill is being directed downward, sadly.

People who are concerned with South Sudan to function as a healthy state and peaceful nation, should throw some extra focus and attention on who lives in "J1" and what he does there throughout the day. Does the president really plan, works and execute the functions and duties of the president as stipulated in the country interim constitution? What are his daily schedule, his long or short term developmental projects, daily mission to implement his national vision "if he has any" to transform the nation and the country? What are his economic plans, security plans and so? We seem like we are in a country without a clear vision of what it is all about or the direction of where it is heading but above all does the president really love his all nation to an extent he wants them to be better, developed, prosperous, peaceful and united? if, so, then why all this cry and blood in the land

Some have blamed Riek Machar excessively for not helping the president when he was a vice president for 8 years. I find this as scapegoating and inaccurate accusation. As vice president of a troubled president, I believe Mr. Machar has done his best and the little positive progress that was being made appeared to be his because when he left or forced out none was ever realized again but all degraded downward and just imagine working in a system where its real elephants are but in disguise stalking your policies and preventing them from fruition until his frustration reached the peak and decided to go opposite the Kiir's way.

Now with the cheering Kiireen and Tabaneen all but drumming that Gen. Taban Deng Gai will but bring what Machar never did. Alright, time is our judge in this but I must tell you this, this ship named South Sudan been in the hands of it captain Mayardit for 11 years, are you telling there were never good people who worked with the president if we exclude Mr. Machar? if so, then why we are here, at the point of nowhere. Mr. Igga and other were there and still before Taban. Our objective as South Sudanese was not to fight on the presidency, this is not what we liberated ourselves for, but to enjoy a free, dignified lives in our country and this is for sure does needs a functioning president, a national leader with love for all his nation, with clear vision and national transformation agenda. I don't deny that Mr. Taban is trying to inject some brains in that "J1" only that the guy has entered from the back door and there are serious doubts whether his "injections" will ever make the already deformed system to be reformed works or its dead man walking alive again. Well, presumably, Taban himself may end up with his boss in his endless coma, a Taban cannot help a Taban. God saves South Sudan.

October 26, 2016

In a Nutshell

Why tribalism seems to be stronger than nationalism in South Sudan despite the fact that we supposed to do better as an independent nation and country? Our excuse when we were part of Sudan was that the successive North Sudanese dominated regimes have used tribalism as a tool to divide and rule the South but how about now? Why tribalism seems like it has grown wild and stronger marching to mess this beautiful, wealthy and promising new state and nation? Why and who is feeding it and why?

Tribalism as a tool in politics of South Sudan is not something new; however, after December 2013, it became the deadliest political tool ever in the history of this nascent nation and this partially due to the fact that the normal reaction of our politicians when caught in the midst of the political competition is that they run to use and mobilize their tribes whenever they sense and smell a political defeat from their political rivals. This is exactly what happened in December 2013 between Salva Kiir and Riek Machar and its aftermath that triggered the bloody tribal massacres all around the country. Since tribes are the pillars that forms this tribal nation, any policy or approach that pit these tribes against each is but a sure policy of total destruction which any responsible politicians should by all means, stay away from such a destructive approach. But says what

However, the competition for political power doesn't end with Tribe (A) Vs. Tribe (B) or vice versa but within every each of this tribes there are another fierce struggle for leadership and political power even though most often we pretend that we in the "one tribe" are united and having it all sound, in fact, the reality says the contrary. However, since the competition has taken tribal shape and direction, it is worthless trying to act as you are not included. Those who thought they are innocent and have no business in this tribal competition and wrangling were and unfortunately the "innocent victims" of most of the ethnic fighting throughout 2013 up to the present. Ethnic based hatred and fights don't spare anyone, they have no other eyes that's sees what is behind ethnicity, if you belong to this tribe no matter who you, you are in, sadly.

Well, despite all that, the "national heart" of South Sudanese hasn't finally departed most of us even though the tribalists have done their ugliest deeds trying to drain us from every drop of it. Since 2013, South Sudan has been a field of tribal annihilation and those warring tribes tried their best to cause the maximum harm to each other, exercising all sorts of atrocities and crimes against humanity, from ethnic based massacres, rape, castrated boys, villages set ablaze and whole cities razed to the ground and all that.

The "national heart" of South Sudanese will prevails over tribalism even in the absence of national leaders and prevalence of tribal leaders; The political and social evaluation of South Sudan could prove to be bloody and complex and time bond, however, sooner or later, we will discover the greatest blessing ever is our nation and our country and not our tribes. Part of this process is happening already. Politically, the competition within one tribe can lead to weakness, divisions and then defeat by the rival tribes who in contrary could have possibly maintained their internal cohesion and strength, picking up the runaway clans yet to use them against their own others. Well, in this and surprisingly, it looks like some sections of one tribe do prefers not to be dominated within their own tribe but willfully feel at ease to be dominated by the rival tribes in the name of nationalism and patriotism. The dilemma is neither the government of South Sudan or Its opposition movement seem to be any better when it come to this approach and as long as the competition for political power is on, tribalism in South Sudan rather than nationalism, will be the political ladder for quite a while.

The good news is that, the competition for political power within one tribe could be a new political breakthrough and could play a balancing factor. Those who are not content with the domination of some groups or clans within their own respective tribe could opt out to form new alliance with their rival tribes or to be "traitors" in the very eyes of their own, well, what disadvantages tribalism is an advantages to nationalism, don't get me wrong. So the defection that we have seen and which has been a two ways phenomenon is but a sort of reflection of that apart from opportunism and job or promotion quests.

All in all, the best South Sudan we all dreams about won't be attained through tribalism but through true nationalism and I doubt that the power houses who dominate either the government or opposition are capable of bringing a national platform fit enough to build a national state for all South Sudanese irrespective of all their diverse differences. If not now, then possibly through the next generations or a miraculous leadership falling from the 7th heaven.

October 29, 2016
In a Nutshell

I am fueling no war ya Natureboy Justices M. This war won't stop with or without me or my writings. It is a war fueled by injustice and people have to defend themselves, their lands, families, rights and dignity. If you are truly keen in stopping this war, talk directly to Kiir, Malong, Kuol Manyang, Makuei Lueth, JCE and many who are leading this war either in the open or behind the scene. Last April, Dr. Riek Machar tried hard to stop the war but what he got is a slap in the face and the real masters of this war restarted it and returned us back to square one, unfortunately.

Those aforementioned powerful figures are the masterminds of this war and are the people who have the keys to bring this war to a halt, the injustice and the suffering of our people. Now you and the likes of Garang Gong, Peter James Wurak, Borjiok, Nebi John and the rest of your Facebook Kiir propaganda squad are heading the wrong road, coming to your victims, labeling them war-mongers, anti-peace and hate inciters but in fact you just want to silence us, prevent us from supporting our helpless people (even with sympathy words here in Facebook) and letting the world know of the injustices against our people, their sufferings and how to minimize the chances of possible genocides since and when the national capabilities of the state of South Sudan (Political, Economic and Military) are in the hands of the few tribal, power-sick and irresponsible leaders, who think based on their ethnicity or tribe, uses and abuses the military, authority and executive powers of the state to advance their tribe's interests and welfare, subjecting others tribes to all forms of injustice.

By doing so, your wish is to hit two birds with one stone, performing all the crimes of injustices and run away with that too, come on folks. Nothing wrong of being yourselves, the drums and the propaganda machine of that killer machine in Juba, disseminating all that cheap propaganda in order to beautify its murderous face but the irony is your expectations of the victims or their families to be numb, defend-less, passive and helpless. That's absolutely not happening. You can't be the one oppressing the people and in the same time the one expecting them to be reaction-less, you can't play it both ways.

When the injustice in its all forms is no more in our country, the war will also be no more. So please stop this cheap game and focus on how you can stop injustice engulfing our nation and country, this will bring peace, justice and reconciliation rather than that it is not Chuar's writings that's fueling the war or the empty rhetoric of peace or the far-from-reality, one nation - one country empty cries that will bring peace. I know some people who fail to understand the objective and philosophy behind my writings "In a Nutshell" or those who have vicious personal intentions who want to score some cheap personal and political scores but this is far making me stray from the point I am trying to make and hence the "In a Nutshell" is here to stay with its noble cause and objective and until it saw the united, prosperous and peaceful South Sudan it is aiming to. Don't accuse me without prove or evidence which simply you can make here by quoting me "fair and honest" and since all I writes are all published in the open. The "In a Nutshell" is collected as a book and it is all there in bookstores and Amazon. Accessed by your national security guys and with some of them disguised as my Facebook friends. Our problem is not because there is no truth in what we write or say, our problem is that it might not meet some people's interests or it get manipulated, twisted and misused. But we can't submit to that otherwise, the change that we seek for South Sudan to be a better country won't happen. My expectation is a constructive criticism and an intellectual debate on relevant issues of our country that's far from characters' assassination attempts or names callings

October 31, 2016
In a Nutshell
Hang on Federalism

A real federalism may save us from the evils of our own and send each of us to his/her paradise spot since we have proven beyond any reasonable doubt that we dearly love our clans, tribes, and hometowns more than our collective nation and country. Well, nothing wrong with that and particularly at this primitive phase of our nationhood development lifecycle. let us take it at ease, one step at time and accept the reality of the nature instead of trying to jump the "must pass" needed process that we must undergo to be a matured nation, with or without a supervision of a good mentor(s) (leader(s)) be that Salva Kiir or Riek Machar, however, our miserable situation reflects a troubled an infancy phase that might need a very responsible, smart and with a wide loving shoulder and truly skillful human mentor who understand and master the art of bringing up a growing infant such as South Sudan. Alas, our current mentor "leader" been hitting north and south in a rare confusion since 2005, when that giant named John Garang left us in a time we needed him most and adding salt to the wounds, he left us without preparing any of those used to be his close associates and subordinates to fill in his big shoes in a time of unexpected emergencies such as the ill-fated Hilocaptor that has cut his life short leaving the nation orphaned

Well, don't worry that much, because nature always takes its course, whether we decided to heed to it or we tried to out-smart its guts by avoiding its prescribed 'learning the hard way" journey through blood, skulls, and skeletons until we are convinced like it is happening now. Well, a good, learned and farsighted mentor could have avoided us all that before it did hit us this hard and still doing so. Our leaders seem to be ruling a nation they never knew anything about because if they do, from the very inception of the independence, precisely July 10th, 2011, they could have formulated a roadmap forward, or a working substance for this nation to live and co-exist in peace and harmony, prospers and take its place among the nations of the world and particularly when it lacks anything but a right and responsible leadership. They could have forecasted ahead of time and saved us from the ton of tribal conflicts and fights since 2005 and predicted what it would be like the return of a nation traumatized by a more than 23 years of bitter war, suffering of all sorts, in IDPs and refugees' camps, a nation that was shaped by all forms of survival techniques Nevertheless, one of the fundamental question directed before the independence to our current leaders and the SPLM/A who also undertook the liberation task and is yet to be a government, was whether they were ready to rule, build a state-nation from these diverse 64 tribes who has more in common, however, needed a leadership and formula to either form the best homogenous nation on the soil of Africa or disperse in warring tribes should they meet their bad luck under a wrong leader and leadership. Their answer was a strong yes, condemning the doubts of the world as another conspiracy against Africans' competency or the capability of ruling themselves.

Unfortunately, the doubts of the world were in place and the same liberation leaders and movement came to be the one proving them right and worse than that sinking and drowning deeper in the ocean of failed rule and failed nation-state building bid. Going back to the point on why I think as many other why federalism is our best hope and sorry if it takes a long U-turn. Real federalism, and not a manipulated one but a real fair and honest federal state of South Sudan, is the answer to our governance dilemma, resources distribution, wealth and power sharing leave alone that it take away the fears of land occupation and grabbing by our very own the powerful strangers, people who concentrated the political, economic and military capabilities of our national country into their hands, acting as it is theirs, doing whatever they want under the slogan "we have liberated you and this country and we are free to do whatever we want and think" and I know that it is sickening to unbelievable extent knowing how we are cheaply wasting the country we have paid for so dearly, to have the same wrong concepts we fought North Sudan and hence coming around to marginalize and commit injustice against our very own this time in the name of tribe superiority and mightiness, that would be a total madness but again, let us accept the reality of growth in absence of right mentor and leader. We part of Africa and Africa is not America nor it is Europe, where tribes are no more, but Africa, as a matter of fact, is the continent of tribe-structured societies and hence most if not all of our socio-economic, political and cultural systems are based on our tribes' norms and systems and accordingly, we can't jump the growth process nor any of its phases, at least not overnight and not in South Sudan context since nations' development and growth are like that of human being, it is a gradual process with many phases throughout its lifecycle, with each phase shaped by its own characteristics, behaviors, degree of maturity and of course degree of immaturity.

If the ruling elites fear federalism because they see it as an attempt to channel the control of power and resources of the state from current center they tightly control and direct at their will then let them be ready to accept federalism forcibly and after the "the learning the hard way" because the reality about this country demand federalism as a system of governance and as a system that will ensure South Sudan and South Sudanese to live in peace, justice, and harmony. If some of us fear federalism because they lack adequate resources, then let them not worry, because, in the federal state of South Sudan, the weak in actual sense will be the one having the attention of the federal government and the federal resources, what count is the way we will collectively design the federalism system for the benefit of all of us and to complete each other. Federalism will minimize the feeling of injustice currently engulfing our country due to fear; each one of us will feel less threaten by dinosaurs of power, tribalism and corruption that compete to control a consolidated power, resources, and wealth in a tribally dominated center and where the national capabilities of the whole state is directed to be used by the dominant tribe(s) as of now. Federalism will feed our unity and not the other way around as some claims that it will weaken our unity instead, in fact, it will minimize the tribal and communal conflicts and clashes in the absence of land grabbing, tribal competition, and greed. It will encourage development from one home village toward the center, however, the federalism that I mean here will need a delicate work, done by all the stakeholders, in good faith and noble objective, far away from the tendency of manipulation, marginalization, and exploitation of other. Taking into consideration the long-term, sound objectives of the people of South Sudan which if worked out diligently and right, its long-terms outcomes should be a strong united federal state of South Sudan and where the South Sudanese identity will gradually replace the tribal nature of this nation. Well, it is a matter of time and of course a matter of good leader(s).

November 14, 2016
In a Nutshell

After spending millions if not nearly a billion of US dollars and considerable efforts that lasted three years of lengthy, complex and difficult negotiations to achieve the ARCISS peace agreement and which Kiir finally unwillingly signed on August 26th, 2015, alas, in July 2016, the same Kiir and his regional and international allies decided to waste all these huge efforts and financial resources to abrogate the very peace they have been singing and dancing about, traveling back and fro from Juba to the various parts of the world just yet to destroy it at all costs and at its very implementation hour. Fresh as yesterday, I still remember how Juba was playing with all the cards and delay tactics to buy time and humiliate the SPLM/A-IO in a series of delay tactics starting with their disagreement on the selection and the size and then later the arrival date of SPLM/A-IO advance team and subsequently, the departure of SPLM/A-IO top general Gatwech Dual and his team and that row of the types and size of weapons they should bring to Juba. Well, in a rare endurance and political maturity founded on the keen willingness to achieve a lasting peace and to bring an end to the destructive war, the movement leader Dr. Machar, finally arrived on April after overcoming a series of humiliation tactics and upon arrival, he was also humiliated even further by accommodating him at isolated suburbs of Jebel Kujor without an adequate working office or suitable residence as a FVP.

Nevertheless, this or that, never discouraged the SPLM/A-IO and its leader Dr. Riek Machar from choosing the ARCISS roadmap as the best political compromise we have at hands so far to achieve a lasting peace in our country. The ARCISS agreement was not only expensive in terms of the political and diplomatic efforts waged extensively at all local, regional and international levels and rendered towards its success nor in terms of the huge financial resources poured into its various processes but mostly in terms of the humans cost that has made it possible and reachable. It is estimated that nearly 100,000 South Sudanese has died either directly in combat zones between the two warring SPLM/A-IO and SPLM/A-IG or indirectly through war-related causes, hunger, and various diseases. With such cost in all aspects of this conflict, the least expectation of any sound minded person is that those who were/are behind its implementation, should by all means and efforts make sure that the ARCISS must and should be cost-effective, that's, it should pay off all the efforts and resources put into it throughout 2013-2016.

Well, not really and never would that be the case in South Sudan that is ruled by people who themselves haven't known its value nor the value of its people's lives who have been systematically dying in unbelievable masses since 2005 and in worthless tribal wars. Nor would that be possible in South Sudan that its death and troubles have become a booming investment to the very region it is poorly delivered and tightly imprisoned. The ARCISS could have meant a lot in terms of settling many fundamental national grievances and injustices here and there whether in terms of constitutional reforms, the overhauling of the decayed and dysfunctional governance systems or institutional restructuring or achieving equity in distribution of national wealth, resources or power sharing and which without no real peace can't be acclaimed. The

ARCISS is the gateway of South Sudan, the resource-rich country to be permanently stable and in peace and prosperity with itself before its neighbors and where it will undoubtedly take its right place among the nations of the region and the world.

However, Juba seems to be still going to school to learn that political stability can't be achieved by trying to sideline, destroy, isolate and weaken political forces with huge political base and military might such as SPLM/A-IO. It is a simple math, it will cost more destroying the SPLM/A-IO than the cost of implementing the ARCISS neither you can't write off realities and facts with few sips of whiskey or just by sinking your brain deep into the sand of ignorance and delusion, in fact, sooner or later you will face the same realities and facts unchanged. This is exactly what happened in last July 2016 madness, it was an attempt to weaken, destroy and isolate a giant political elephant such as SPLM/A-IO, but it failed miserably and more to that, it is about to fire back.

To achieve a lasting peace in our country, we must heed to the fact that all political forces, big or small, must work together to achieve consensus on the future and direction of our country and this won't be possible without the right environment and democratic atmosphere that encourages dialogue and debate nor it will be possible without a real change at heart in Juba regime. The ARCISS must be revisited, made effective and efficient again and implemented. It must be made cost-effective if at least by putting it into reality and effect if we would be all spared from being stupid. Stupid people who have wasted such a huge investment that has cost nearly billions of dollars, 3 years of tough negotiations and most importantly 100 thousands of precious lives without any cost-effective deliverables. Let us think again.

December 15, 2016

In a Nutshell

Dec 15, 2013, is not just a sad cloud that has passed over the South Sudan's sky for a split second and that would be forgotten and forgiven with rosy words and mere wishes. It is a real disaster by all the meanings of the word. Its mental and psychological wounds would stay unhealed for quite a while, its socio-economic and political consequences will be hard to overcome as it is evident in our ailing economy, problematic and fragmented political leadership and in the destroyed social fabric, trust, and confidence among our communities, but more importantly the rebuilder or the fixer can't be the same destroyer. Someone else with a better approach and a better appetite may do better.

But of course this would be far from happening because the current political leadership is not ready to relinquish the seat of power in Juba leave alone the political theatre and hence it is not likely that we see any initiative aimed at bringing a new political actors or climate rather than a prescribed political formula and process that keeps both the dysfunctional political oldies and their tight grip on the gates and the corridors of power and as we have seen in the proposed president Kiir's national dialogue and reconciliation.

for the people of South Sudan, leaving agonies and bitterness of 2013, 1991, 1983, 1984 massacres behind is what we are all about because our existence and destiny as a nation are so connected with that and because we will be doomed if we choose to permanently dwell in our bitter past. However, the problem here is not our inability as a nation to forgive or forget but the problem lies on our opportunistic political leadership, which at hours of its political defeat will hurriedly revisit every detail of the bitter past, manipulate and fuel them to be what keep them in power and political space at expenses of our innocent populace and country. The current conflict as we all recall started within the troubled house of SPLM and ended as an ethnic feud and bloody tribal war that crippled both the nation and country and in which each one of us has sided with their tribal leaders no matter whether they are right or wrong and which is also our collective weakness as a fragmented nation vs. our manipulative political leadership.

When it comes to true national dialogue and reconciliation, Kiir is not the one that should dictate the process since the ARCSS that he abrogated in July recommends just that. The victims' families represented by SPLM/A-IO-Dr. Machar were gradually coming to enter into supervised and gradual reconciliation and healing process with Kiir's political base if things went well. But see the irony and contradiction of a failed political leadership, after forcing its partner in the peace process out from Juba, it is here winding in the same spot it refuses last July. What a confused political leadership? Which ARCSS and SPLM/A-IO does he really means in his speech? That one of Tabaneen or the one with Gat-Machar?

However, let us not lose hope in the oneness of our country and nation because of poor political leadership despite the fact that, the timing of Mr. Kiir's speech raises one's eyes' brows, let examines his speech as part of the political process and not necessarily a binding agreement. Hence, I can say there is much positive side to Kiir's speech if it is for real and not for political consumption and buying time purposes. Kiir seems to have finally realized that the conflict is no more a Riek Machar's rather than it is a deep socio-economic and political conflict with deep underpinnings that are destroying the nascent nation. Those underpinnings must be thoroughly addressed, tribalism, land grabbing, nepotism, corruption, lack of nationally balanced and professional national army, law and security forces, the tribal mindset we have, the sick tribal and prejudice we place above our collective common interest as a nation, lack of independent institutions, the legislature, executive and judiciary are all but in president's and his security henchmen control, these are few among many that must all die for South Sudan to live. South Sudan, need a re-engineering in all aspects, socially, economically, culturally and politically for all the ills to leave us alone. There is a need for us to know and understanding who we are in order to formulate what is best for us, we can't just randomly and blindly roam around and expect all will be OK. We need a working sound socio-economic and political system, a thriving culture of success and more.

Such a re-engineering endeavor will be impossible without the know-how technocrats who the system in Juba sees as the real threat instead of real knowledge that they can use to re-shape and position South Sudan for better. 90% of what Kiir has said in his speech has been predicted and discussed by various South Sudanese intellectuals in their different discussion forums and social media outlets but they were all given deaf ears.

I wish the proposed national dialogue is genuine and broad in its scope and that all political forces including SPLM/A-IO-Dr. Machar, Dr. Lam Akol and all the political forces are considered and invited. I have no doubt that Kiir will resist his removal by force and use every destructive method to frustrate that and in the same note, the de-organization and fragmentation in the various opposition forces are at their worse high, it seems the opposition has now turned into empty voices in social media without any real organization at ground. While the suffering of our people is mounting, Mr. Kiir in his J1 is untouched and undisturbed. If his proposed national dialogue is inclusive, held in neutral place and supervised by neutral bodies, secured and genuine, and as part of the political actors, the SPLM/A-IO proper should consider participation.

December 17, 2016

In a Nutshell

Don't feel defeated neither frustrated, the Dec 15, 2013 was not an equal war or a matched fight between us and Kiir, it was an unequal fight between our poor unarmed citizens and what we regarded as our national government with all the capabilities and resources of the nation and as you may recall, not in the history of Nuer tribe that an enemy ever inflicted such huge losses to ours leave alone getting away with it. This is evidenced in what our people did as a reaction to Juba brutal regime massacres to their families which in a matter of few days, they have captured most of the greater Upper Nile region from Kiir genocidal militias and if the war was managed and executed well, Mr. Kiir could be by now, very much a gone case. Well, no regrets anyway, we still have him by the horns.

The Nuer tribe must learn from the Dec 2013 if they didn't learn through their troubled past with the SPLM/A and now with the SPLM/A dominated government which successfully executed an ethnic war in the last three years, leaving the members of the Nuer ethnic either killed, uprooted, displaced in IDPs or refugees' camps or reduced them to indecisive beggars in their government. If the Nuer can't learn or would be still insisting in their culture of underestimating threats then be ready for much worse massacres than Dec 15, 2013 and likely genocide on the way, as the SPLM/A seem to be in complete control of the government and the resources of the country leave alone its unbalanced composition while it is being funded and empowered by a national budget and resources as a national army. As we know, the current SPLA, neither in its chain of command nor in its manpower reflects a national army by any standards, it is a pure single ethnic and region militias and that's why there are high risk and a real threat of ethnic genocide. The formation of a national, balanced and professional army was the fundamental aspect of the peace agreement which Al-Tabaneen, blinded by greed and selfishness, have evaded. Well, the real dilemma of Al-Tabaneen when they betrayed the SPLM/A-IO is that they went to the enemy while they are bare feet and without a single soldier that may protect them if Kiir decided to slap them on the face anytime leave alone asking him to implement a thing in what they still think and call peace agreement. Evidently, it been more than 150 days, and with "Zero" implemented from Al-Taban-Kiir peace agreement.

Well, when Kiir and his army chiefs, Malong Awan and Kuol Manyang obtains fighter jets, hilocaptor gunships and the most sophisticated weapons, the Dec 15, 2013 will be like a tiny drop of blood in a full pool of blood. The current approach of Kiir and his army chiefs and their security forces is to build a huge and well equipped tribal militia in the name of national army and use it to manifest their dictatorship and accordingly, given the tribal approach and mindset, tribal hatred as a substance and ideology for such a political project, genocides and ethnic massacres are not just likely but will be sure things. We better read this terrible mindset and stop it before it is emboldened to a very dangerous and clear danger.

Nevertheless, when we write facts and predicts possibilities some people jump on our necks and accuse us of being tribalists or war mongers, which is an attempt to fight our role in making our people aware and informed of what the fragile situation in South Sudan may lead. On the other end, it is an attempt of re-enforcement of the injustice and the status quo. As Mr. Kuol and Malong continue to build the SPLA ethnically and militarily and equip it with the deadliest heavy weapons, the likelihood of genocide is greater than ever and as long as our opportunists Nuer are continuing to be the catalyst and accomplice in this scheme, the future of Nuer and other 63 tribes will always be haunted by fears, death, injustice, domination, and oppression.

As South Sudanese, we must resist by all means the formation of an ethnic state, army or government, neither for a Dinka, a Nuer or a Bari dominated state or government or army, we must forge an inclusive South Sudanese state, government, and army. A South Sudanese state with a solid foundation, where the rights of all are enshrined in an inclusive national constitution and laws, where liberties and freedoms are for all South Sudanese, we must never allow an ethnicity based state and if some are fooling you that this is about Riek Machar, get over it, it is about you and your children and grandchildren. We must resist an ethnicity dominated state.

December 19, 2016
In a Nutshell

I may call a spade a spade with the SPLM/A-IO when someone like CDR Koang Ranley decides to join Juba regime and not that I may join Juba regime at any capacity but definitely will roam around searching for any viable political movement that may share with me the objectives

and the vision for South Sudan. Our hero Gen. Koang
Ranley is doing a great job despite the logistics and
technical difficulties his forces are facing right now and I
must admit that the clips of the videos posted here by
Chuol Ranley II are the ones keep me in hope that no
matter what there will be light at the end of this tunnel that
the SPLM/A-IO is currently passing through rather than
that I see a movement that is dying slowly even though not
surely. Well, I know some of us think that it is like
committing sin when pointing to the weakness of
SPLM/A-IO in general or its leadership in particular,
however from performance and effectiveness concern, I
feel that the SPLM/A-IO of 2013, 2014 and 2015
respectively is not the SPLM/A-IO of 2016 and that the
latter is in strange type of ineffectiveness and lack of
efficient leadership.

Since July, 2016, when the Chairman was evacuated to
safety successfully, I was expecting a performance that is
better than before as the situation should dictate, however,
in contrast, I haven't seen any notable success neither in
political or military front, in fact, it been a setback
followed by another, culminated in the kidnapping of his
own spokesman Mr. James Gatdet Dak, a vital asset to
himself and the movement. The kidnapping of Mr. Gatdet
Dak reflects within SPLM-IO leadership a lack of ability to
read or anticipates the next moves of the enemy or any
analytical body that analysis what enemy could do next, for
example we knew Taban and Lol will be on the offensive,
protecting their new jobs and political power but the
SPLM/A-IO never had a counter plan to evade their
plans. More to that, our brave young heroes who did the
highest heroism by taking the Chairman to safety, are still
stranded in Congo and it been almost four months without
seeing a concrete plan for their relocation from Congo to
the liberated areas under SPLM/A-IO. Sometimes, I
wonder whether Dr. Machar has resigned and retired

politics without notifying his political base or maybe he is the one who have crowned his brother in laws and close aides Taban Deng Gai and Ezekiel Lol Gatkuoth as his hires in power, fearing a backlash from the disgruntled SPLM/A-IO political base or a rejection from Kiir's political establishment. This trend is being re-enforced by seeing people who I haven't thought of betraying Gat Machar at any situation, someone that I know best, like Mr. Hussein Mar Nyout, this time and around, have said to be in that herd, well I still have my doubts and don't believe it yet, anyway, in both cases, making it work as a coup is definitely the right recipe.

Ironically, the Chairman left Khartoum to South Africa instead of Pagak even though the suggestion that Mr. Machar could be given a political asylum by South Africa surfaced when Mr. Machar was still in Khartoum and this would also suggest that Mr. Machar out of fear of being held as a political hostage by both Juba regime and its regional and international collaborators shouldn't proceeds with his plan to visit South Africa and instead to Pagak while he could revive his movement and reclaim his place on the political table. However, defiantly or maybe his health conditions dictated for him to overlook the sure and clear consequences of such a risky visit. Well, after almost three months, Mr. Machar is still in South Africa but ironically enough was the scenario of his attempt to leave South Africa to Ethiopia and then to Pagak and which the same rumors circulated his forced return to South Africa, arrest by Addis Ababa and Khartoum or expiration of his visa, well whether these are smokes with or without fires, something fishy is being kept away from the public and we could be the stupid who are swimming in the wrong direction while it is all a done deal.

Since July, 2016, the movement has been in limbo and ineffective except for the small pockets of resistance in

Equatoria region which were in dire need of support and re-enforcement but with no avail and until it is now being cornered by massive government forces to extinguish its fires, no such re-enforcement or support haven't reach them. Realizing the leadership vacuum and ineffectiveness of SPLM/A-IO, I suggested a month ago in Facebook status posting that if the chairman's health condition dictated his stay in South Africa, that's fine but clearly Mr. Machar can't hold the movement a hostage and hospitalized too and that at least he should restructure the movement on new efficient basis, appoint an effective deputy that should take care of the movement efficiently while he is following his medical treatment. Well, a month later came the appointment of both movement's new deputy, secretary general, and foreign committee chairman, however, since then, the movement still very much in limbo and inactive.

Organizations, be them social or political, are like human beings and if you are expecting them to grow and flourish, they must be watered on daily basis, must be put to work, and they must be put into efficiency and effectiveness but most of all they must have the ability to retain their current clients or members and the ability to attract new ones if they have to be classified as efficient, successful and progressive. Well, the moment you see organizations have ceased attracting new members and the norm become the existing members leaving the organization one by one or in groups, this is the moment you should, as the leader or the manager of such organization, have to think twice and find out why your organization is in declining and shrinking state and if you are truly still willing for your organization to compete with others in the s, product or the political markets, you must fix what is missing, enhance your performance and boost your competitive advantage in order to thrive or survive, however it seem the SPLM/A-IO is losing its members and instead of finding what is wrong within its foundation and performance, it is giving its former loyalists and members a nasty goodbye, yesterday was Agel Machar and tomorrow will be another big fish, well, let us find it out, something might be wrong with the waters of SPLM/A-IO and not necessarily the fish or vice versa and it have to be confronted head on for a possible healthy come back. The failure of SPLM/A-IO has a very immediate and future consequences and at your comfort zone you aren't aware of them right now, you or your children will definitely feel the heat in future.

It is worth noting that and despite their betrayal and backstabbing sin to SPLM/A-IO, both Taban and Lol Gatkuoth have been at consistent and tireless work, day and night, pulling the carpet from beneath Dr. Machar and if you are a keen observer to the turnouts in the SPLM/A-IO meetings and social media support leave along the regional and international support, you may also have observed that there is a steady decline of SPLM/A-IO role and place at both political and diplomatic ends. Given the current ineffectiveness and lack of activism within SPLM/A-IO proper, Al-Tabaneen are for sure heading to a win and as you know, in politics, there is no impossible nor there is either permanent enemies or friends. As for the SPLM/A-IO under Dr. Machar, this is a failure and degrading indicators and if the leadership of SPLM/A is awake by any extent, they must take charge and put their movement into work one more time otherwise blame it to the movement inefficiency and prepare yourself to the bitter taste of defeat.

December 21, 2016

In a Nutshell

You never know when a dictator may have encountered a change of heart at the middle of the night and hence decided all of the sudden in the morning to confess his sins and crimes to his very own victimized nation, overcoming his selfish and tribal ego and asking for forgiveness from his many victims. However, the case of our dictator Gen. Salva Kiir is a little quite different because first, he hasn't confessed yet in a manner that put him in his right place as a man in charge of this country where all the shortcomings should be blamed to him and hence he is the sole responsible of whatever happened in this country as its president and not because he is a Dinka as some of our tribalists always thinks. However, that wasn't the case and even Mr. Obama, the president of United States, a country that is founded on respect of humans' rights and dignity, was more courageous than Mr. Kiir by taking a moral responsibility of the persisting slaughter happening in South Sudan even though he is not the president of South Sudan. While both men may have the same Nilotic ego given Obama background only that Mr. Kiir couldn't swallowed his like his counterpart, Obama, and decided to present his as short of full confession, indirect and warped in confusion.

However, for those who know Mr. Kiir, his action of coming forward and asking for forgiveness wasn't an easy one or his initiative for the conduct of what he termed "National Dialogue" wasn't even easier. Mr. Kiir could be a very humble man whose heart is being visited sometimes by his true own self and sometimes by sensations of the power wants and illusions and between the two we have the Kiir that can be tough today to maintain his power and the Kiir that can be human tomorrow when he realized that his actions of keeping power are no longer, human. Well, power is seductive, corrupt and dangerous if you have gained it by default and without any good objective of your own, that's, apart from the high chance of being influenced, changed and corrupted by the power itself or by your inner circles or those power seekers. You got to have your own objective of what to do with power and above all the morals and principles capacity before the allure of power and the negative inner circle got the wheel from you.

Nevertheless, we have received the proposed "National Dialogue" with open arms and hopes and we have envisioned it as a broad dialogue between various and diverse sections of our nation, tribes, warring political forces, leaders, and an inclusive process that leave no social or political entity out or excluded. Simply because such a broad dialogue is truly needed in this very much divided and fragmented country as a result of the three years bloody civil war. Our country is totally destroyed and our nation has been in serious suffering in all aspects intensified in the last three years, death, hunger, diseases, malnutrition, uprooting, and displacement. However, the worse is that we are even heading further deep down into the path of destruction, death, and ethnic fragmentations than ever before and culminated in the high likelihood of ethnic genocide occurrence.

Grievances of all sorts are the source of our political wrangling and most importantly are the ways they are being addressed which in most cases are wrong recipes that instead of answering the said grievances, they just add extra fuel to the flaming fires. Ego, ignorance, tribal and militant mindset has been at the center stage of the provided failed solutions and since the dawn of our independence, the missing truth and the underpinning of our problems or what could be the right prescribed solutions, were provided, discussed and debated in many South Sudanese or international political and social forums. However, the ruling elites who are mostly military figures and violent oriented due to their military backgrounds and the legacy of 22 years of war for the liberation have chosen military solutions, violent, coups conspiracy theories, and physical elimination of their opponents and hence has sidelined any prospects of peaceful, democratic dialogue at all levels.

Traditionally, the South Sudan of our forefathers and mothers was founded on peaceful family and communal dialogue, whether at family level, social and tribal or the political level and that's why we have inherited South Sudan and its diverse communities very much intact, living side by side and united and if the current approaches to our tribal disputes or political ones was the one been there since then, there couldn't be such a thing called South Sudan by now, we could have finished ourselves in merciless tribal massacres, genocides, and uprooting. Everyone who have read or heard president Salva speech may at first impression been inspired that Mr. President at last, has come back to his true self and sense and that he has learned from his own fatal mistakes that drove his nation and country to this miserable state. Well, they said that the devil is always in the details and until we saw his appointed committee for the proposed national dialogue packed with the same people who in a way or another, were the cause of the conflict, part of massive financial and political corruption, part of the wide spread atrocities, same people who been watching the country falling apart but their focus was their positions and more looting of the country financial resources apart from the fact that the committee didn't reflect in some of its structure the inclusiveness and diversity of our nation and as we have mentioned above that addressing grievances requires the grieving communities or the social or political entities to be included so their version of stories can be heard.

Another concern is the venue of the national dialogue which the president has dictated to be the insecure and the politically intolerant Juba. No single political opponent or party or even those journalists or human rights activists who tried to simply state their different political opinions or objection on some human rights-related violations who doesn't know the certainty of being harassed and intermediated, jailed, forced disappearance, kidnapped, tortured and thrown half alive beside graveyards or at worse shot by unknown gunmen, these sad realities and encounters make Juba ineligible to be the venue of true, diverse and broad "National Dialogue". Sadly, enough, neither the promises and words of Juba regime can't be trusted anymore, given the bloody July in which the SPLM/A-IO was lured into Juba city to implement the ARCSS and in which the regime seized the window of the "benefit of the doubt" that was given by SPLM/A-IO and the opportunity to build the broken trust and confidence during the ongoing civil war. However, to Juba, it was another smart tactic, show of power, raining the SPLM/A-IO with rain of bullets on earth and skies, in an attempt to wipeout its leadership and its small protection unit which has finally led to the collapse of ARCSS peace agreement

Well, if the regime truly need credible "National Dialogue" as well as its outcomes, then some changes must be made in terms of assigning a neutral body to supervise the dialogue as well as inclusiveness of the grieving communities, change of dialogue venue to a neutral site where all participants can feel secure, safe and free to state their grievances and opinions, otherwise, there is nothing new about this proposed "National Dialogue" which in its current structure has nothing national about it nor it will produce any tangible outcomes.

January 5, 2017
In a Nutshell

The killing of Major Gen.Tangyene is meant to create internal fighting within the Nuer community in particular and within the SPLM/A-IO in general. It is a well-calculated conspiracy and I argue our people to be vigilant and above it and instead to be ready to expect uglier conspiracies that will try to put them against each other. The ugly turn of this war is being shifted to be a Nuer vs. Nuer war by our collective enemies but when we all became weak and losers at both camps, this is the time we as Nuer, will realize that we became slaves in our own country. Al-Tabaneen, who are now very much convinced that this fight is all about power, positions and turning Riek Machar to a non-violent dove while himself and his community are being constantly killed and slap on both cheeks 77 times. They forgot that this fight is for our people's dignity and freedom and sadly they are set to fight their own community and do all they can to settle this fight on their own side, in fact, Kiir side. Well, I pity them as they have no choice, partly because, they already committed the gravest sin against their own community and the return to the grace they have lost is likely impossible unless they came with a miracle, hence they are more active and effective to dismantle the SPLM/A-IO and win.

Since they have no army, Al-Tabaneen in collaboration with Kiir are working harder to destroy the SPLM/A-IO from within, pit the political masses against each through confusion and propaganda, buying some with positions and money and they are in a constant day dreaming and prayers if the SPLM/A-IO military units would come to divide and start an internal fight which will send some defeated ones to their direction. They may have a plan to eliminate the heavy weight military figures such as what happened to Gen. Tangyene even though we still lack the details of his sad demise. Was he really part of Dr. Lam Akol recruits? How? I haven't come through such news and development and someone should show me a piece of information of when Gen. Gatwech Chan joined Dr. Lam Akol.

Sadly, enough, the circulated photo of his dead body in social media seems to be of a person who was tortured and beaten alive before he got executed. That's why the details of his death must be unearthed, investigated and analyzed but of course, the Nuer will react madly as usual and then he will be forgotten tomorrow just like the demise of Gen Titu Biel Chuor, who also was lured out of UNMISS and killed mysteriously in cold blood. Our enemy could be within the SPLM/A-IO and the details of Tangenye's death if known could vindicate us or confirm our doubts and suspicions. The whole conspiracy seems to be well planned rather than a coincidence and look at that bogus letter which the African Press website claimed to be a congratulatory letter from Dr. Riek which is pure propaganda and lie. Isn't that part of the conspiracy? How and from whom the African Press did obtain such a letter otherwise who runs and publishes African press? Which side are they?

Well, the question of the hour is who is next? Apparently all these generals; Gatwech Dual, Mabour Dhol, Gatdet Yaka, Gathoth Gatkuoth and many other SPLM-IO political activists could be in the line of the blacklist. Juba evil political coalition is moving and moving fast than you think but then the question is: is there anything the SPLM/A-IO is doing to counter the plans of the enemies? Such as beeping up the security around the SPLM/A-IO political and military leadership as the trend that the enemies are going to use the death of Gen. Tang to create confusion and conspiracies so they succeed in putting the Nuer or SPLM/A-IO against each other. The devil is at work while you are busy blaming and dividing yourselves even further. Irrelevant!

We always cautioned that the enemy is within and it has been within since the inception of SPLM/A-IO and despite our writings consistently that the SPLM/A-IO has been penetrated from within and at its highest echelon of leadership even before the advance team and leadership arrived to Juba but no one was heeding to our warnings because the same elements has surrounded the leadership feeding it with ill advisory and confusion until the SPLM/A-IO arrived to this miserable state. Despite the many wake-up calls, happened here and there, the trend that we should wake up when worse things happens reflects a poor state of minds that are detached from the reality or that underestimate the enemy abilities, capabilities, and ill intents.

Nevertheless, we find ourselves crying and in pain when we lost an experienced fighter like Gen. Gatwech Chan on the wrong hands and wrong circumstances because the loss of these experienced fighters regardless of what we thinks about them, is real below to the community and since they are being bought and seduced by politicians between time and another to fight for the politicians' contradictory and controversial political projects given the fact they are experienced fighters who since the inception of the liberation been roaming the bushes of South Sudan bare feet from north to south and from east to west and the chances are that they end up on the wrong side just as Gen. Tangyene. However, one would still rise an eyes' borrow how come did Gen.Tangyene and Gen. Mabour Dhuol ever ended up on one side with Gen. Olouny and Dr. Lam Akol given the hostile history and legacy between the four since the days of Anyanya 2. Possibly that they still could be allies against Kiir but not in one army and this is one of the reasons why Olouny kept his own army, a pure Choli army. Well, still irrelevant.

While destroying the SPLM/A-IO is the booming business of the day and with Juba ready to pay the local, regional and international hitmen millions of dollars more than it can feed its hungry populace with the objective of eliminating the SPLM/A-IO role and leadership wherever they are, it is likely that success will be theirs if the only thing the SPLM/A-IO will be good at is crying, complaining, blaming and the empty threats. Well, in parallel, while the Nuer themselves are very much occupied with their own many wars, the enemy is preparing to come and finish the little that is left from here and there. How are we making foolish of the second largest community in South Sudan if not the first? Still irrelevant!

Sadly, we have a problem as Nuer people; our intellectuals are also too selfish and with a clannish mindset and tend to see the situations and plans of the enemies with shortsighted lens that's see no far than their short noses and hence failing to see the big picture and the objective of divide to rule policy which in its reality it has no good Nuer but the one that serves the enemy and finishes his own. This isn't about Riek Machar ya comrade, get over it before you are gone in confusion. Gen.Tangyene has a legacy of 1% wrong and 99% right only that we tend to remember the 1% wrong. Rest in Peace General.

January 7, 2017

In the year 1995 I remember the killing of all these
Generals Manyiel Kueth, Koang Benpiny, Lok Riek,
William Nyuon Beny, Elijha Hon Top, Joseph Tot Weay
and countless other under the same pretext that they were
killing their own Nuer. But the killing still going on until
now. The Killing of Gen Tangeyne won't stop the killing
in the Nuer society just as the killing of Samuel Gai Tut,
Abdallah Chuol Deng, John Kulang Puot didn't. Neither
the Nuer have achieved the objective they have been
massively dying for since 1982, isn't the time we think
twice and review whether things are alright with us? What
is killing us is the confusion that some seem to celebrate
and don't want to be addressed! Those are the masters of
our problems and death! #Chuarezkoff's

January 7. 2017
In a Nutshell

Of course, each has a right for self-defense, however, it is
sad that Gen. Olouny is showing his sharp teeth and
mighty power to the same people who have rebelled
against Kiir like him in order to liberate Malakal and the
rest of South Sudan. Gen.Yohanes Okuic, Gen. Tangienye
and Dr. Lam Akol are not the enemies; the enemy is the

one who is occupying Malakal right now and in the very watch of Mr. Olouny and this is where he should use his sharp teeth and mighty power. I understand that there is a question of why we all should join hands under a powerful and diverse SPLM/A-IO as people who rebelled against Kiir tyranny regime and then fight as a collective force until he is gone instead of each one of us forming his tiny, small and clannish movement of his own that neither will defeat Kiir nor single-handedly will affect any change.

Not long ago when Dr. Lam Akol being holed up in the Kiir's country and in a house arrest until he safely left the country as a minister and subsequently resigned from the short-lived TGoNU government, formed his new rebellion movement the National Democratic Movement (NDM) and instead of joining hands with his Engineering colleague and also political rival Dr. Machar since days of the SPLM/A second split, he decided to go his own way. Well, partly because he may have thought that Dr. Machar has proven his failure and that the public opinion in SPLM/A-IO and the rest of the country is charged with frustration and definitely are looking for an alternative leadership that can lead the suppressed masses into victory through a national, inclusive movement that represent a unified national program for change and with the notion that Mr. Riek Machar won't deliver a thing and look at him where he took us given the last bloody ordeal which broke the SPLM/A-IO's back into pro-Kiir group or Al-Tabaneen who replaced Machar and loyalists and the pro-Machar group who were chased away from power into the bushes of Equatoria until later and luckily arrived safely to Congo, well, Mr. Akol may have seen in himself the alternative to Machar and his NDM as an alternative to the embattled SPLM/A-IO.

Therefore, since his resignation, Dr. Lam has chosen to advance his rebellion quietly and smartly, infiltrating the ranks of disgruntled SPLM/A-IO generals and the frustrated political masses as well as the wide South Sudanese political and military players, however, a bit of success was of his. Probably, he may have approached Gen. Olouny but failed to convince him to leave the SPLM/A-IO beside the two men may have their mistrust back in the days in 2005 or so. What still a puzzle is whether the ill-fated two generals, Tangyene and Yohanes Okuic have arrived to any deal with Dr. Lam or is it a mere suspicion given Gen. Olouny keen reading to what Dr. Lam is all about and hence moved fast to cut Dr. Lam's claws before they grow any longer. However, since both Dr. Lam and the SPLM/A-IO are here because of Kiir, one would wonder whether isn't the right thing to do for both is to cooperate and fight Kiir instead of annihilating each other in that way we have seen and where their top Generals' dead bodies are on shameful display in social media. Well, their masses and supporters would be more cheerful if those were Kiir's generals instead of their very own.

Given their engineering background, both Dr. Lam and Dr. Riek could have avoided this sad ordeal that resulted in the loss of these experienced fighters and could have engineered a better approach, a better alliance and a better coordination against Kiir since July and on the wake of their exit safely from Kiir's sure killing zone and at least if the two men can no longer accept to be called deputy of any of each, they still can form a better alliance which they needed most in this critical time.

In the same context, the former Western Equatoria governor Joseph Bakasoro and the former Yei Commissioner and countless other opponents to Kiir's government could also joined hands with the already fighting SPLM/A-IO, making it a national movement with a broad national base and agenda to offer an alternative to

Kiir exclusive regime and as I mentioned above that opting for creation of tiny, clannish and ethnic based political movements and armed groups for the sake of being called a Chainman or the C-in-C isn't the solution for South Sudan problem or what will defeat Kiir or affect any change. What South Sudan really need is an inclusive national leadership and movement for a better change that is better than Kiir and his regime in all aspects and if these collective tiny ethnic movements in opposition can join hands, they could win the fight against Kiir at no time.

However, I understand that there are many political barriers and mistrust between the leaders of these tiny political and armed in opposition groups. Differences that ranges from conflicting selfish interests, leadership ambitions and approaches to how the conflict can be addressed and settled. Well, diversity and differences in ideology and political opinions are the norm in any organization be it political or social, however there is always a common ground where all these entities can meet and agree to work on achieving a common goal, for example, removing Kiir from power by force or peacefully defeating him in election but going all the way separately, and single-handedly makes defeating Kiir a mere illusion, in fact, he is going to crash each one at his own corner and squeezes the jelly out of each eyes at no time.

Well, if the collective objective really is to provide a better system of governance, build a better country with institutionalized democracy for all South Sudanese and a brighter future for our next generations then one doesn't see a reason why we could not come to an agreement and a common ground. All that South Sudan need is not resources but a good leadership, a unity of its people, peace and security and then we are all set. I believe Olouny needed Gen.Yohanes, Dr. Lam Akol and their men in his fight to gain Malakal back to the Chololand as much as Dr.

Riek needs Bokasaro, Dr. Lam Akol and vice versa for each to win the case against Salva. Otherwise, let us stop talking about regime change in the absence of an effective and working strategy, it would be just a waste of lives and efforts.

January 18, 2016
In a Nutshell

Kiir Mayardit wants us to be stooges and political opportunists in our country, dividing our land as he wishes and as his own cake where he sells every piece as a state to the titles, positions and money worshipers on the basis "do you want a piece" and where in fact, our political opportunists and hungry positions seekers, money worshipers will without a shame, grab the offer they can't refuse.

Unity and development should be the criteria behind any geopolitical division to our land and people but in Kiir states' scramble none of the two is a reason, in fact, weakening, isolation, and marginalization of some South Sudanese are the real objective behind this more states political strategy. When South Sudan seceded from North in 2011, our main problems were not tribalism nor were it more states neither was it Riek Machar. We have fought for 23 consistent bitter years and voted overwhelmingly with 98.8% referendum vote to have collective freedom, dignity, liberty and a dignified life for all of us, South Sudanese, and not for a selective single tribe or clan.

Well, even though if we needed more states and more counties given the shaky political and administrative structure we inherited from Sudan, such a process would be a people-based process and for the objectives of an inclusive political representation, fair distribution of resources, an inclusive power-sharing and many others apart from the fact that any such geopolitical division to our land and people must be preceded by an extensive research and feasibility study that should identify the cons and pros of such a sensitive process. Are the new states sustainable and can they stand alone in terms of resources? What are the immediate and long-term effects of this process to the unity of our people? What are its socio-economic and political benefits or consequences? Is it fair, equal and above all is it inclusive and doesn't marginalize a South Sudanese or whether it isn't giving some favored group a greater slice than the rest. All these are part of the many concerns must be answered before Mr. Kiir rush to his SSBC TV and announce his unilateral decrees.

If you think the Kiir creation of more states scramble is about economic boom and political representation then think again because not too soon to forget that the creation of 28 states in 2015 has added more death than it has added more dollars into our ailing economy and that it has injected hatred into the hearts of our people, fragmented our people even further and destroyed our unity and centuries old, beautifully woven social fabric.

So what is the essence of adding more salt to the wounds? Well, we don't mean more states or counties shouldn't be created if the need necessitated such a request but in real democracy, policy making is people centered, where people are involved and actively engaged and decide through their elected representatives or through direct referendum votes where they have their own opinions and say considered on crucial issues such as this 'more states and counties creation". Alas, Kiir has robbed our political power as well as the rights to decide and participate in our political affairs and destiny. He is the executive president, the legislature, the judiciary, in other words, he is the police, the C-in-C of tribal militia, the policy maker, the judge, the banker and worse of all, the unknown gunman.

Well, just like any future president, Mr. Kiir can't be the center of our universe, he surely has a mandate, limitations under the constitution and he surely will leave one day even if he rules for his lifetime but our land and identity as South Sudanese will always remain. Hence, our common ground and center stage of everything should be being "South Sudanese" and while the presidency is a leadership position, meant to be people based and to be the pulse and heartbeat of the people, albeit and since then, Mayardit and his bandwagons have made the presidency a tool of clans and family members' empowerment and self-enrichment through public funds and public positions. They made the country a bargaining product, where they have given themselves the ultimate rights to divide and sell it as they wish, to destroy it and to uproot its inhabitants at will. Every president has a mandate and a term and Mr. Kiir went out of both on July 9th, 2015 and ever since he has been operating illegally and not all that, he has been abusing and manipulating the powers of the presidency in a way that keeps him and his drummers in power as long as they want.

With the recent creation of more states decrees, General Kiir has not only successfully brought the fight to our door steps but also smartly switched the war to be fought in our own families, between us and our uncles, fathers-in-law, brothers, sisters and cousins while at the same time he has secured his tight grip on power and to use the resources of this country as he wish. The country is in acute hunger and needs more food not more states but in Kiir country, a hungry man has to think first what he will have for the day before he thinks of 'Kiir must go" and this is why Mr. Kiir wants the war and the hunger to just be the routine and accordingly the "Kiir must go" must now be a Diasporas' song and not Kiir-own-made hungry stricken populace.

January 19, 2016
In a Nutshell

The abrupt replacement of Mr. Gai Raim by Gen. Gony Billeu before even he could be sworn in as a governor of the newly created state of Akobo hasn't come out of the blue nor the appointment of Sultan Konyi as a replacement of Buma state governor Baba Median but all indicate that Kiir and Al-Tabaneen are opting for the military option to bring the areas under the IO control and particularly the Lou Nuer area to their control and hence they need military figures that will do just that and not only that, military figures with a bloody records and blinds in loyalty to the Beny- Mayar. Well, Both Gen. Gony Billeu and Gen. Majok Gatluak Thoa have unquestionable loyalty to Kiir and while I don't recall much about Gen. Majok Gatluak Thoa having been in the military operational tasks during the ongoing civil war, I don't doubt his keen willingness to carry on any task Juba will ask him to do and which is to bring his Bieh state to the control of the government on a bending knee.

As for Gen. Gony Billeu, his loyalty to his boss Kiir as well as his ruthlessness as a military commander is also unquestionable as most of us may recall that Gen. Gony was the man who's under his command, the region of Upper Nile was brought to complete rubbles and Malakal to the city of skeletons and ghosts under his many offensive and defensive, capture and recapture wars with the SPLM/A-IO. I have no doubt Gen. Gony will do the same to Akobo if not all the Lou Nuer region. As for the appointment of Sultan Ismail Kony and its connection with the whole scheme is obviously logistical to the invasion of Lou Nuer and as a good collaborator in the upcoming destructive strategy to our people. The military operations will need a closer base to the Lou Nuer area and also a friend who's also a good enemy, rival, and hater to the Lou Nuer people and area, this may all apply to Sultan Kony given his troubled history and rivalry with the said region and people and on the basis "the enemy of my enemy is my friend" Kiir and Kony are now friends against the Lou Nuer and will use these kids 'Gony and Gatluak" against their very own. Well, don't bid on it, I may be wrong.

Mr. Taban want to consolidate his newly found glory and power and the Kiir-Taban agenda for the year 2017 is to bring most of the areas under IO control to theirs and which means the people in those mentioned areas must be ready for the upheaval and the bloody war that is underway. There are many children, families, elderly in Lou Nuer area and I believe the military preparations for such a strategy are complete and our people shouldn't be caught off guard as we know that Lou Nuer area has been mostly secure and stable due to the united front of our people which deterred and frustrated Juba many attempts to destroy and control it and unlike IO stronghold Bentiu which was brought to annihilation because of the disunity of their leaders and its people. During the 4 years bloody civil war, Lou Nuer remained largely untouched and haven't been destroyed and this is also another factor that is moving many of our enemies and wishing that it also should be brought to rubbles and its people killed, displaced and uprooted.

The destruction of Lou Nuer area will also symbolize the end of IO and the Nuer last defense stronghold and by that Kiir, Kuol and Awan along with their Nuer accomplices may toast their champagne bottles and celebrate the end of the threats to Kingdom-dit where everyone will by then, obedient to the domination system on a bending knee. It is worth noting that after Malakal was destroyed and much of the Upper Nile was largely destroyed and deserted, Gen. Gony Billeu and his Governor Kun Pouch were immediately relieved and that Malakal was annexed to a new state in which both Kun and Gony were neither citizens nor have the right to be employed, sadly. This scenario is coming to repeat itself and after their successful wars on their own areas of Akobo and Uror, both generals Gony Billieu and Majok Gatluak Thoa will surprisingly discover that and after they blindly uprooted their Lou Nuer people from Akobo and Uror that both cities will be declared by Salva a non -Lou Nuer cities just as was the case of Malakal and if you are truly a Lou Nuer you know where these cities are going to be annexed or given to.

Well, I may be wrong but tell me one reason why I would trust Mr. Kiir policies and plans? Simply, I have no reason to trust Mr. Kiir and to believe that what I am seeing is a contrary to what he really wants to do which if we give it the benefit of the doubt we can say "Mr. Kiir is trying to bring the country back to stability and peace, ensuring inclusive political representation by creating more states, replacing wrong people with right people, and all that and that let us go with him a mile or two". Well, this would be the normal situation if trust exists or there was any drop of it not drained by Kiir himself. But can we trust Mr. Salva after all this bloody ordeal? If not, then my above narration could probably be what is going to happen!

January 21, 2017
In a Nutshell

If Gen. Kiir himself doesn't know who he has appointed as a governor of Waat or whether the name of his new created state is Bieh or Waat then isn't this enough to tell you this whole conspiracy is a cook of Taban Deng and

Lol Gatkouth and just to bring the destruction to Lou Nuer area in their fight against Riek Machar? Well, don't be surprised, Kiir is imposing his own peace, his own choice of stooges against the will of our people and under the threat of militarily offensive and invasion and want us to accept that or face the imminent consequences. Stripping Riek Machar from political influence and power, the vast popular support base to Reik Machar must be dismantled and the Nuer must be bought with positions, money and if need be made to accept that by aggressive force. Taban and his crew must be made a winning reality by all the means necessary and much of the year 2017 will be consumed in wars of that nature and it seem it is starting with Waat and Akobo.

So Waat and Akobo are not until this hour accessible from Juba as Gen. Kiir admitted and calling on his new appointed governors of both Akobo and Bieh to militarily invade them and make them accessible. But, Mr. president didn't have the audacity to ask himself whether this would be the case had he had the courage to implement the ARCISS peace with Riek Machar last July and that whether Waat and Akobo and like many other areas under SPLM/A-IO proper control would ever need a military offensive to make them accessible. So Mr. President has destroyed the peace meant to stop the war in July only to come in January and with a different face to enforce the peace of his own through war, pathetic isn't it? How come, Waat and Akobo are not accessible when both Kiir and Taban drums and sings days and nights that Mr. Machar is over, a done deal and parked like a car in South Africa and that peace is here and emphasizes that the SPLM/A-IO and IG are all in the government and that ARCISS peace agreement is alive and being implemented. Shouldn't that mean we are in peace and all SPLM/A-IO areas are then normally accessed without any need for any military operations? Nope, don't be surprised again because Liars won't notice at the same time that they just proved, in a way or another, that they are just, Liars!

Well, if not for the destruction of both and the confusion of general public, making Waat and Akobo accessible won't rescue the Kiir government from its many woes, economy and security at most nor they could have been given a priority but out of jealousy and hate to Riek Machar, Lou Nuer a stronghold to Machar must be punished and also be brought to rubbles and Mr. Taban and Lol Gatkuoth are coming to wage the war against the children, women and elderly of Lou Nuer through the lost sons of the area, Kun Billeu and Majok Gatluak, aiming at turning it to another Bentiu and Malakal and while at the same time calling Riek Machar a violent-monger and that he should denounce violence and come to Juba and live as peaceful citizen. Isn't that a peak of contradiction? Alas, for the sake of being called FVP, Mr. Taban is being used to stab and destroy his community and when they are done using him and the rest of the crew, Mr. Taban will come to term with the harsh reality that it is Paul Malong or Kuol Manyang that will succeed Gen. Kiir while he will be dumped and kicked out of the presidency, in a way or another, and the rest of his crew disowned a bit by a bit because their terms of use is no more.

Who would deny this as part of a well-planned JCE political project that is being implemented phase by a phase and where Mr. Kiir is just a show face and facilitator. However, the attempt to invade Lou Nuer militarily will work surprisingly different and deliver opposite results than the ones expected by our enemies. Lou Nuer isn't the obstacle to peace and since Kuol Manyang brought his Ugandan mercenaries in 2014 to defend his hometown and people in Bor which happen to be a strategic gate to Juba, the JCE establishment seat of power, the Lou Nuer youth, white army and SPLM/A-IO has been very much in defensive and protection positions and hardly managed to attack Bor or initiated any military advance towards Juba.

Well, should Kiir and his accomplice Nuer insist on the destruction of Lou Nuer area and try to bring it to annihilation then there will be for sure a war of who should control the Lou Nuer area and while our people will be displaced and uprooted after they have been very much enjoying security and stability under the protection of their gallant youth, white Army, and the SPLM/A-IO , the area will be a new open grave to Kiir's Mathiang Annyour since Taban-IO has no single battalion that he could claim as his. The nature of Lou Nuerland is not a helping factor to Mathiang Annyour to stay there even for a month, however, and since the mission is to destroy the villages and displace the villagers who have been very much secure and in peace than those in Mr. Kiir own sin city, Juba, the war won't be avoidable nor its final result will make Waat or Akobo accessible or bring Kiir-Taban appointed governors to stay in Lou Nuerland. The sad ordeal is, out of clannish jealousy and selfishness, the Nuer came to destroy the very peace that was meant to empower them and give them their right share in the country. Salva Kiir wouldn't dismantle the ARCISS peace without some of Nuer weakness and complicity, some didn't handle seeing their own Nuer in better positions than seeing Salva Kiir on top of them neither they were able to handle having their own plate than being beggars in their own country, albeit they still talk about Nuer attaining political power, how is that? through begging? Pathetic!! Political power can't be attained through begging or political prostitution.

Lastly, the invasion of Lou Nuer militarily could bring the whole region to a new face-off and neither Pibor nor Bor or other surroundings will be spared because we will unearth every enemy that has a role in the invasion of our people and land and make them pay twice. Kiir must not be deceived by Taban Deng and Lol Gatkuoth that the invasion of Lou Nuer militarily is a mission possible and if I was in his position I will rather explore other peaceful political alternatives than waking up the beast in us.

ABOUT THE AUTHOR

Sandro Chuar Juet is currently a PhD candidate at School of Business and Technology with emphasis on Project Management and Northcentral University, USA.

Founder of Nile Computer Solutions, an IT and Computer Technology Solutions provider small business based in Omaha, Nebraska-USA. He has been managing it since 2007 up to the present

Holds Masters of Science's degree in IT and Project Management and Bachelor of Science's degree in Information Technology and Business Administration (Honors)

A graduate of the prestigious Khor Omer National Model Secondary School-Khartoum

This is his second book, a collection of opinion articles that he has been writing since the 2013 outbreak of civil war in his home country, South Sudan. The "In a Nutshell" is a timely analysis to the events and the role of the local, regional and international key political players, where Mr. Sandro offer his opinion and predictions. Both books can be purchased from Amazon

At Khor Omer National Model Secondary School-Khartoum, Sudan 1988

During My Masters graduation at Colorado Technical University 2011